ALWAYS A NEW

BEGINNING!

A CONVERSATION BETWEEN BROKEN CATHOLIC SPIRITUAL WARRIORS

RONDA CHERVIN, PH.D.
PROFESSOR OF PHILOSOPHY AND
DEDICATED WIDOW

DAVID E. DOWD
REPENTANT CATHOLIC POET, FORMER
INSURANCE UNDERWRITER

En Route Books and Media, LLC
St. Louis, MO

Make the time

En Route Books and Media, LLC
5705 Rhodes Avenue
St. Louis, MO 63109

Cover credit: TJ Burdick

Library of Congress Control Number: 2020946126

Queries may be sent to chervinronda@gmail.com or
davided.dowd@gmail.com

ISBN-13: 978-19524-643-17

DEDICATION

To all the Broken Spiritual Warriors
we have met and hope to meet again
one day in heaven.

WHAT'S INSIDE?

1.

WHY WE WROTE THIS BOOK

"Behold, I am doing a new thing; now it springs forth, do you not perceive it? I will make a way in the wilderness and rivers in the desert." (Isaiah 43:19)

RONDA:

So why would I, the writer of so many books about spirituality, decide to write one more?

I think you'll be surprised. I was.

Retired from fifty years of being a professor of philosophy, a speaker on Catholic TV and radio, and a writer, I am living with my granddaughter Jenny and her family. For the first time in more than seven decades I have absolutely nothing I have to do except, finally, to become a saint!

Dietrich Von Hildebrand, the Catholic philosopher who, sixty years ago, helped bring me from being an atheist to the Faith, proclaimed that there is an abyss between being an ardent Catholic and a saint. Well, that abyss I planned would be crossed in my old age by Jesus levitating me up to the ceiling, St. Teresa of Avila style.

Four years into retirement I have not yet levitated.

So, I am always looking for the missing piece.

As a dedicated widow (see my website hosted by En Route Books and Media at https://www.rondachervin.com for an explanation of this vocation), my rule includes daily mass, rosary, liturgy of the hours, the mercy chaplet, and one-half to an hour of quiet prayer. I have a spiritual mentor I consult weekly. I also live simply, giving whatever funds I can easily manage to do without to the poorest of the poor via the Missionaries of Charity.

So, what's missing? You want to visit and see? Well, I get inordinately angry about five times day – mostly in my head. I hurl denunciations against heretics about ten times a day – mostly in my head. I anxiously try to avoid all suffering by fretting about little and big crosses instead of entrusting them to the permissive will of God.

And all this in spite of writing books that greatly help others to become more holy in precisely the areas where I so often fail.

So, about a year ago, my good spiritual friend, David Dowd, told me about a home retreat book, *The Artist's Rule.* One of the themes was new beginnings. Suppose we worked on it together via phone conversations, Dave offered. I was eager to try.

David will be describing his insights from that book in his introduction, so here I want, instead, to tell you only about how the very idea of 'new beginnings' began to challenge me.

What? Even at age eighty-two, could I begin anew? Well, Jesus didn't say "Be ye perfect" and then add, but not after seventy-five. Then you can just slide into purgatory. And in my quiet prayer, Jesus is always urging me on to holiness.

I define, holiness, by the way, as having nothing but love in one's heart: joyful love, sorrowful love, struggling love, reverent love for God and the Church…but not pockets of resentment, despair, and anxiety.

Before we go further, a note about the term 'broken spiritual warrior' in the title. The word 'warrior' is used in Confirmation to stir up the teens to realize that they are called to fight for their faith. Many older Christians use it to describe a spirituality which is not only rooted in contemplative receptivity but also can be stirred by a battle with one's sins and defects.

The documents of Vatican II speak of "the universal call to holiness." To answer that call entails struggle with the evils within and a passionate desire to love God with one's whole heart, mind, soul, and strength, and one's neighbor as oneself.

So, I like the image of David and I not only being spiritual friends, but also broken spiritual warriors.

How about the word "broken" in the sub-title? A Benedictine Abbot once said that most of us want to see the spiritual life as a rush up a trail to the mountain top. Instead, it is more as if we start up the trail, fall into a thorn bush, and get stuck. Then Jesus comes down the mountain and rescues us. Then we start again up the trail, a little further along, and again fall into a thorn bush…The trail is spiraling upward, but we can barely realize it, because we are so surprised to be stuck in thorn bushes over and over again.

In looking for a new beginning we, the authors, are not pretending that we are spiritual masters. Instead, we are broken spiritual warriors, hopefully nearer the top of the mountain than when we started.

On still another preliminary matter – it is important that family and friends don't think that this New Beginning, as a book, is directly related to each of you. You may appear on these pages or in a photo, but you shouldn't think that some passing remark is a sign of the way either of us writers views you in our whole relationship.

Back to why we wrote this book. Once David and I started dialoguing about our insights coming from the home retreat, I noticed that his new beginnings also inspired me and vice versa. So, being such a non-stop writer over the years I thought, "these dialogues of ours could be a book so that we could share these insights with others."

As I begin writing *Always a New Beginning!* with David, my prayer for myself, for him, and for you, readers, is this:

"Come Holy Spirit, help us to truly be willing to sacrifice our time and energy in the battle for holiness. No matter what our failures in the past, open us to new beginnings."

DAVE:

"Quiet, your judging mind, grasshopper."

In working on the *Artist's Rule* retreat together, this thought was one of the highlights for me.

I had moved to the Fingerlake Region of Western NY to be near my son. I was sixty-eight years old and had lived a busy, broken trail of a life. With the grace of God, I had sought meaning in living my faith through fellowship and relationships with friends in Distance Running, Pro-Life, Street Preaching, and Traditional Latin Mass circles.

My broken trail of a life was cluttered. My work and personal life was marked by emotional struggles, lost jobs, a broken marriage and, when I felt a failure and embarrassment to my family, suicidal ideation.

My being hospitalized in Middletown, Connecticut, in 2011

provided me a "New Beginning." But I had to face myself, first. I would need eight years of intensive sustained DBSA (Depression, Bi-polar Support Alliance) group therapy. Led by my friend, Alan Rosenthal, this therapy brought me out of denial to learn the relationship between acceptance, self-management, and freedom!

But what to do with the rest of my life?

My work had included insurance underwriting, student loan collections, and fundraising for a religious order and a Pro-Life group.

In 2016, while I was in treatment, I reconnected with Ronda. We, originally, met in California in the early 90's. Now Ronda was teaching a course at Holy Apostles College & Seminary in Connecticut. I enrolled in her class. We often had luncheons afterwards. She was delighted to discover that besides being a strong Magisterial Catholic, because of my successful treatment, I was also into psychology. She also loved to meet friends of mine who were into street preaching and friends who were enrolled at the college via Distance Learning.

My family, so supportive in the lean times, was in the process of loving me back to life. My son, Dave, tenderly, accompanied me through my third hip adjustment (which occurred while I was in Rochester, NY, for Father's Day in 2016.)

Then, in December, 2017, when I had to have a second hip replacement on my left hip, my son, and my brother, Tim, approached me a few days after surgery (while I was groggy and in my hospital bed). They said, "the time has come for you to live nearer to Dave and his wife," dear Gwen, "in the summer in New York, and nearer to Tim and his wife," dear Maggie, "in Florida during the winter."

Little did I know I was on the threshold of another 'New Beginning.' My past-life included pretty cool involvement with poetry, running, music, and pro-life circles. I was ready for retirement and finding stimulating friends and sparkling conversation! Retirement sounded pretty good!

I was staying in touch with Ronda when I made my move in December, 2018, to just south of Rochester NY, where my son and his family live.

So, quietly, does the Holy Spirit move. He placed a book, *The Artist's Rule*, in my hands while I was browsing in a Trappist Monastery bookstore in Geneseo, NY.

I eagerly discussed my new find with Ronda Chervin. And I asked her if she might like to read this together.

So, from my writer's nook at Vitale Park on Conesus Lake in NY, to my writer's nook at Fort Pierce Inlet in Florida, we did work on the retreat together!

The relationship we formed in reading *The Artist's Rule* became the ferment of the project that became *Always a New Beginning*!

Now, we are about to come together and celebrate something I could not have imagined when in group or in rehab....

The path to new beginnings!

For the Reader:

You might make a note here about your initial reasons for reading *Always a New Beginning!*

2.

THOUGHTS FROM THE MARSH
DAVID DOWD

"For the promise is to you and to your children and to all that are far off, whomsoever the Lord our God shall call." (Acts 2:39)

DAVE:

Ronda asked me: "Looking back at our working on the home retreat based on the book *The Artist's Rule – a 12 Week Journey* by Christine Valters Paintner, what would you say is the key insight or experience you gained from that spiritual exploration?"

So, in reply I remembered that one day, while reading, I came across this phrase: "Imagine there is something you are being called to, something good."

I found myself slowing my thoughts down. I went for a walk and allowed myself to drift into the silence of the moment.

I thought of the practice recommended in the home retreat of the boundary awareness of being open to your inner monk and your outer artist...

RONDA:

Hold on a moment, Dave. Let me explain those terms, "inner monk" and "outer artist" to our readers:

The inner monk is a term used by the author of *The Artist's Rule* as a metaphor. Monks physically live in monasteries where they leave the busy world outside to spend most of their time in contemplative prayer, often living on farming or a craft.

The inner monk refers to the interior life of a person who does live in the world but wants to become more contemplative. Example: instead of spending spare time after work and family duties on tv or games, such a person will go to a little chapel area in their homes or out for a walk to think and pray.

The outer artist is a term devised by the author of that retreat manual to help the participant get in touch with each one's often buried artistic talents – to make a little drawing of one's favorite tree, for example, or to make dance movements while praying.

DAVE:

Now let me return to my story about my highlight from *The Artist's Rule* home retreat.

Walking and breathing in a new way, as I breathed, I sensed the time of day, observed the season of the year, and acknowledged my age. In this way, I would have a frame of reference to better absorb given moments in my life, more deeply, more uniquely...more as my moment.

RONDA:

Yes, you've got me thinking. I'll come back in a few moments.

DAVE:

Here is a poem I wrote about this new beginning:

ENCOUNTER WITH YOUR INNER MONK
AND OUTER ARTIST

DAWN

> MONK (Inside)
> Dawn breaks, breathe in, fill your lungs.
> Awakening.
> Your eyes and throat, now, clear.

> ARTIST (Outside)
> A fresh breeze on Spring morning!
> Buds slowly open.
> Multi-colored petals.

DAY

> MONK (Inside)
> Refreshed oxygen in blood.
> Sensitive in touch.
> Now your mind is thinking fast.

ARTIST (Outside)

Sun rays from high in the sky.

Ears of corn growing.

Blossoms adorn new fruit.

DUSK

MONK (Inside)

You release and surrender.

And shed some worries.

Now you can prepare for sleep.

ARTIST (Outside)

Flocks of geese are flying South.

Autumn's golden light.

Once brilliant leaves are falling.

NIGHT

MONK (Inside)

Slowly, your breathing pauses.

Contemplate the dark.

Uncertainty? Surrender.

ARTIST (Outside)

Crickets chirp in the stillness.

Moonlight glistens.

Roots flourish, now, in Winter.

Now, you the reader, might try these spiritual exercises:

MORNING

Quiet yourself. Go for a morning walk sometime during the week, carrying these suggestions with you.

- Notice your rhythmic breathing. Feel your lungs swell and then empty as you breath.
- Notice the moment you draw in breath. Imagine this is like the spring time when new life is budding on the trees. When little bunnies are hopping across your lawn. When mother duck is making way for her ducklings behind her.
- You are in your youth. Walking on a path in the woods. Feel the crisp scent of evergreen in the air.
- Sense fresh oxygen flowing into your brain.

This is your morning moment.

MORNING SCENES – SPRING
Photos by David Dowd (aka dd)

Spring buds

Little bunny

Mama duck and ducklings

RONDA:

Recently I moved to a house right near a lake. The sparkling of sunlight on the water has totally changed my mornings. I purposely keep a window clear, without blinds, to see the lake first thing my eyes open. I say a prayer of gratitude for the beauty of the lake God created. I do a deep breathing prayer, partly with eyes closed but often with a little peek at the lake.

Ronda's early view of the lake

NOON

Another day, go for a noon-time walk. Return to your breathing exercises.

When you notice the noontime sun high in the sky, pause. Be aware your lungs are full. When I took the walk, it was summer. The heat of the sun was blazing in the sky. Crops in the farmer's field stretching to ingest the sun.

It reminded me of the prime of my life when I was in the summer of my years. Fresh blood reached the very tips of my toes and fingers.

NOON SCENES – SUMMER
Photos by aka dd

Corn in farmer's field

Abbey of the Genesee

Old Reservoir Road

RONDA:

As a retired dedicated widow, Dave, my highest priority is daily Mass. But my second highest priority is avoiding the cold since my circulation is poor, and I am cold unless it is seventy-five degrees!

As a result, I love noontime when the sun is usually out to warm me up here in Hot Springs, Arkansas.

AUTUMN

Take another walk someday at dusk. The shadows begin stretching across the green grass. The sun rides lower in the sky. Maybe the leaves are turning yellow or dropping from the tree. Your lungs are emptying as you exhale. Figuratively, you are in your middle-age approaching the autumn of your years.

DUSK SCENES – AUTUMN
Photos by dd

Shadows at Vitale Park

Sun disappearing behind trees

Autumn leaves fall from trees

RONDA:

Dusk is not my favorite time of day. I find it a bit depressing. However, since the retreat I made with Dave the outer artist takes more enjoyment in the fading light of dusk. I am advised for health reasons to take more walks. In summer, at dusk it is less hot. That is often when I walk around our forestry area, often breathing deeply in and out - the name of Jesus.

NIGHT

DAVE:

I took this walk in the winter. I noticed my breathing. I noticed a rest at the bottom of my exhale. My body was dormant for a second.

I noticed trees had lost their leaves.

I noticed the snow as winter set in.

This pause in my breath seemed like the somber solitude of death before eternal life. The quiet on my path was mysterious. It led me to seek answers to questions.

Even if it is not winter where you are, take time to consider the elements of winter as you pause before resuming your breath.

RONDA:

As I grow older and older, now I am eighty-two years old, I find night to be inviting, precisely to be more aware of thoughts and prayers. Without the distraction of everything around me I normally see, I can better commend my spirit into the hands of God through the night prayer of the church and through individual, personal prayer.

Here is an example of one such night encounter with God:

Before falling asleep I felt drawn into, "hidden in His wounds," a place of withdrawal from the world.

This state of being felt like what John of the Cross meant in his poem "at the top of the mountain nothing," which I think of as "no –

thing." Or Teresa of Avila's "God alone is enough."

I felt my soul being "sucked into" a kind of peaceful void such that all the human beings I know were distanced, and I was saying farewell. Not in the sense of physical death but of the 'death' of the fierce dependence on them and their approval.

Dear Jesus, one night will be my last on this earth. I want to rush into Your arms. Mother Mary, every day I pray the Hail Mary more than fifty times. There is that petition "Pray for us sinners, now and at the hour of our death." Please, on the last days of my life, may I see you in a vision praying for me.

DAVE:

I love these prayers of yours, Ronda. As I conclude this account of the start of my new beginning, I remind the reader to be comfortable whenever you feel prompted to practice these rhythms of your breathing. This will bring you closer to the mystery of God's living presence and your unique place as He reveals His Mighty Love for you.

NIGHT SCENES – WINTER
Photos by dd

Winter in Vitale Park

First winter car ride

Aged and snow-swept barn

For our Readers:

You have already been invited to follow Dave's leads in this chapter. If you wish, keep a journal using your words, your sentences, to express your thoughts as you find your path in the woods, in your neighborhood, in a city park, on an inner city side-walk or on a lonely beach.

Add photos if you like to take them.

3.

FIRST CHALLENGE

RONDA CHERVIN

"Let us then approach the throne of grace with confidence, so that we may receive mercy and find grace to help us in our time of need." (Hebrews 4:16)

RONDA:

How could I become more grace-filled instead of jerky? That was the question I asked myself considering a new beginning.

"Grace-filled" has two meanings for me. The first is grace-filled in the sense of a graceful dance. I am like this because my twin-sister is a dancer. I loved to watch her dance at home and, later, at performances.

Here is a photo of my twin-sister, Carla, dancing with Veronica, the wife of one of my grandsons (see page 28).

By contrast to my twin's gracefulness, I was a "klutz" – a Yiddish word meaning a clumsy oaf.

Dave, can you tell me something about your feeling clumsy or graceful in your youth?

DAVE:

Ronda, where do I begin?

One sunny day, my mom placed me in a play pen outside in the sun while she did housework. To the sound of barking dogs, she rushed to a window. Then, she grabbed a frying pan and flew to my defense. A neighborhood Doberman Pinscher had jumped inside the pen and was menacing me, barking at me!

My mom was not to be trifled with, but I had fear of dogs for years!

BEAUTY AND GRACE:
AUNT CARLA AND VERONICA

Then there were two concussions.... once on a playground, at age five, I tried a dumb move on a slide and fell, broke my wrist, and got a concussion. Then, a few years later, my friends and I were sliding on a hill behind our grammar school. My sled caught an edge in the ice. I lost control and made a direct hit on the wall behind the school. I was knocked out for a couple of days ... I came to in a hospital.

I evolved into that shy kid who stuttered and shied away from most activities. Luckily, my friends, Gary and Don, made me laugh at myself. My dad and mom and brothers teased when I deserved being teased, and I survived my "klutz" years.

But I was still shy with girls. My first date was with Gail Durocher at the ninth-grade dance.

RONDA:

You are remembering this in a somewhat humorous tone. However, I bet it hurt a lot to be made fun of as a kid. Many have found that to be really traumatic.

To go back to my theme of graceful vs. jerky, the second meaning of graceful for me is to be full of divine grace – God's energy permeating my being with love.

Now these two meanings combine in this way:

Most of my physical movements throughout the day are jerky. By that I mean unnecessarily quick, edgy, bumping into things, picking my finger-nails. Also, most of my emotions are jerky – mixtures of annoyance, anger, fretfulness in the midst of many moments of grace-filled love…And my prayers are often rushed, as if I was in a race to finish first!!!!

So, when I try to improve, I want to work for these changes: doing everything physical slowly; breathing more deeply when emotions get into knots; intoning the Jesus prayer while breathing deeply, and praying formal prayers with slower intent.

DAVE:

Ronda, being in perpetual motion, with what seems like a revolving cycle of "to do's" as my health improves, I sometimes feel like I need to make up for lost time. After hip replacements and eight years of therapy for emotional struggles, I find, often, that as I slip on the treadmill of life, it is because I move through everything too quickly.

During our recent retreat I learned that I need to work harder to slow myself down. I, also, find I need to get outside in nature.

Now, there are two good places where I enjoy writing. I think of them as my writer's nooks.

The first nook is at Vitale Park on Conesus Lake, thirty miles south of where my son lives in New York. And the other is in the Indian River Inlet in Fort Pierce, thirty miles north of where my brother lives in Florida.

As I was saying, Ronda, in times of stress, I find my thoughts speed up. I try to notice these moments and stop what I'm doing and slow down.

I am also remembering additional new practices to manage my thoughts. They include saying the rosary daily. I listen to You-Tube talks by Father Chad Ripperger, an American Catholic priest, theologian, philosopher, and exorcist. I often find peace in these practices when I am settling down to sleep.

These practices calm my, sometimes, racing thoughts at the end of the day. With my history of anxiety, my thoughts in my fallen nature sometimes can become disordered. So, the prayers I just described are my battle plan, as a broken spiritual warrior, to go to war and emerge victorious against my disordered passions.

Of course, we don't always emerge victorious, but good confessors have reminded me "Jesus sees the fight we wage." They encourage me to pick up my sword and my shield and go right back into the battle. I have come to understand this as my sacrament of confirmation at work!

Writer's Nook – Vitale Park

Writer's Nook – Indian River Outlet

RONDA:

Some women I have known tell me about similar problems. In my case, as a new widow, I sometimes struggled with different fantasies in the night – dreaming about possible husbands. Less of that when I became a widow dedicated to Jesus with Him as my second bridegroom.

DAVE:

Clearly, in this day and age, many men and women struggle with lower passions that can become unbridled. This struggle can be fueled by pornography. Porn is such an exploitation of broken men and broken women. An addiction to pornography can intensify as our unchecked passions overpower our reason.

RONDA:

I heard that, these days, indulgence in pornography is the most confessed sin.

DAVE:

My sacrament of confirmation prepares me with the following action plan:

I try to go to Confession twice a month. I love the Traditional Latin Mass, and I try to pray the prayers before communion before Mass.

I pray the English translation reverently as Father celebrates the Mass.

Then, after Mass, I stay in my pew and read the prayer of St. Bonaventure and the poem by St. Francis Xavier.

I also keep prayer cards from the 23rd Psalm from the funerals of my brother and my stepmother in my prayer book.

This might seem like too much information, but I have found these prayers before Mass, praying the Mass, and then prayers after Mass really transform my Sundays into an occasion of spiritual retreat.

RONDA:

That's wonderful, Dave. Of course, you would practice many of these prayers around the Holy Mass as part of your worship of God, but we need to know how much they also brought you graces in the struggle with night thoughts you were so open as to admit.

DAVE:

In my earlier discussion of spiritual warfare, I have come to understand living my sacrament of confirmation places the graces of the Traditional Latin Mass squarely in the battle of sin coming out of my lower passions. Padre Pio reminds us that the rosary is our weapon, but in my experience, the graces from the Traditional Latin Mass are my shield and my sword.

The battle, Ronda, is a hard one. I cannot just turn off my passions. I have to learn to trust, to have faith, that God sees my battle.

In addition, my brain disease of bi-polar includes the component of racing thoughts.

So, I fight a battle where my bi-polar impairment impacts my freedom. But I do battle with the rosary, with the direction provided by priests like Fr. Ripperger, and the grace that comes with my sacraments as my weapons.

RONDA:

The Mass is a gift the Lord provides in many ways. In view of the tidal wave in our times of sexual sins, it is good to bring our struggles with temptation more consciously into our experience of the Holy Mass.

DAVE:

Ronda, you nailed it. We do need to bring our struggles with temptation more consciously to the foot of the cross in our experience of the Holy Mass.

There is so much more to the interior transformation to becoming more graceful than I thought when we started working on this theme.

I need to emphasize to myself the relationship between the graces from the Mass and my own effort to become more graceful.

Well, I think I've made progress.

But I still start each day as a new day.

I still need my first cup of coffee and some quiet time to enter the day. I am so glad I am retired. I can generally ease into the day. But, if I have an early appointment, I still find I procrastinate, lose time, and, suddenly I am muttering to myself and racing through my morning routine.

If I need to drive to a meeting at Church, or a doctor's appointment, heaven help a slow driver in front of me.

My son rides me like a hawk. If I am talking fast when we speak, he stops and says:

"Dad, slow down. You need to get out of your head. You need to give yourself permission 'to just be.'"

In a poem he wrote, he encourages me to sit in the sun ... just experience life through your senses.

If I am driving, and if I become more self-aware of my anxiousness, I think of my late brother, Dan. Once I passed Dan on Route 91 in

Vermont. We were going to New Hampshire. There I was racing up the road at 75 mph. And Dan? He was moseying up the road at the speed limit.

Here is a third mindfulness moment. The other day, when praying, the memory of my Dad behind the wheel of his car impacted me. As an impatient youth, to me my Dad's practice of pulling away from an intersection slowly allowing the sound of the motor shifting gears to guide his acceleration conflicted with my demand to get to where we were going. In my prayer, Dad's practice calms me and so, now, I pull away from intersections guided by the sound of the motor and not by my impatience!

I, also, try to stop to listen to slow, stimulating CD's or Father Groeshel's Rosary CD when I need to slow down.

RONDA:

Here are some of my experiences as I tried to spend a whole week being more grace-filled vs. jerky.

Doing Everything More Slowly:

Every single time I do something more slowly such as walking from the desk to the stove, or taking a slower bath or, especially, eating more slowly, I find myself feeling more peaceful.

Bringing Knotty Emotions to Jesus in Prayer:

I tried not, by myself, trying to untangle, those emotional

responses to everything frustrating in my life. Every time I remembered to immediately bring them to prayer, I would feel better. By better I don't mean that the difficulty was unraveled, but that it had less force to upset me. In the case of an insulting rant I delivered to a family member, after begging for forgiveness, which was forthcoming, I brought it to Confession.

Avoiding Artificial Deadlines:

Due to my husband's disability with severe asthma, my life was extremely busy when I was a wife, mother, and breadwinner. This led to getting everything obligatory done way ahead of time.

However, now, as a retired professor living with my grand-daughter's young family, there is hardly anything I do that has a deadline! So, creating artificial deadlines, such as the laundry has to be done each day, or this piece of writing has to be done tonight, makes for jerkiness! Every time, trying for a new beginning, when I told myself, instead, that I could work slowly without fretfulness at the same daily activities, I felt greater peace.

Concerning spirituality itself, Jesus seemed to tell me this:

"Ronda, you feel terrible that the process of your growth toward holiness is so, so slow. Here is a grace-filled image you need to consider: would it be a more beautiful, graceful dance, if the male comes out to the stage and lifts the prima ballerina up into the air on one hand and then everyone claps and it is over!!! No! There is the slow unfolding of all the steps leading up to that culmination, which for you is Jesus leading you into heaven."

Further, Jesus seemed to say that I need to see Him as the lead dancer to whom I respond. My prayers of inner words or traditional prayers are good, but if I prayed them more slowly, less jerkily, Jesus could insert more grace into them.

With traditional prayers, such as the Liturgy of the Hours, with the many psalms, I felt led by the Holy Spirit to make very simple hand gestures to match the words such as lifting my hands high at the word glory.

Jesus seemed to tell me: Suppose you see Me as the lead dancer and you responding to how you think I am leading you! Wouldn't you become more graceful? All your prayers of words, traditional or newer are very good, but pray them very slowly instead of jerkily rush, rush. Sing and make motions as you pray those words as the Spirit leads.

DAVE:

Ronda, reading your descriptions of graceful living immediately slows me down.

My world of "do this, do that"; be on time for this appointment, record that appointment in my calendar, reply to these Facebook posts, post or comment on my Facebook posts, wolf down meals, ha ha, the nerve ending twitches merging endlessly until I fall into bed after my evening routine of brushing my teeth, taking my meds, etc., seems to be a little out of synch with the grace-filled images I just encountered.

For our Readers:

What forms of jerkiness do you find in your own daily life? What would gracefulness be like for you?

Can you write a prayer, short or long, for what you need from God to grow in grace-fulness?

4.

QUIET ONE'S JUDGING MIND – GRASSHOPPER
DAVID DOWD

And it came to pass that while they talked and reasoned with themselves, Jesus himself also, drawing near, went with them (Luke 24:15)

DAVE:

My mind tends to leap, like a grasshopper, from thought to thought, and subject to subject in conversation. Then, often comes scrupulous self-blame.

For example, sometimes when I read ideas online that I disagree with strongly, like climate change is more important than abortion or the latest Democratic complaint about President Trump, I tighten my eyes and shake my head and feel a squeeze in the back of my neck! Many thoughts are immediately triggered.

Sometimes, I even get upset! Ha! Ha! If I am on Facebook, triggered by my complaint cascading through my mind, I might sit down and fire off a snippy retort and post my commentary on my Facebook page! If I am watching TV, I might turn the channel.

Ronda, if my mind is leaping around like a grasshopper, how do I quiet it?

RONDA:

Good question. I am just like you on this. Having worked on it for many years in Christian anger-management, what works best for me is something like this:

1. Bring the issue to God as in: "God, the Father, You created us with free-will. As a result, people disagree with You on the truth. And we disagree with each other about many matters: ethical, political, or prudential; even about trivia. Help me to accept Your permissive will about this over-arching reality of freedom and difference."

2. Ask myself, "would I rather have robot 'yes-men' around me who automatically agree without a moment's conflict?"

3. Thank you, Holy Spirit, that you have brought me to the truth about the matters being debated nowadays.

4. Holy Spirit, help me "speak the truth with love." Tell me how to make this immediate issue, during a conversation in person, or on-line, or in my head, into something positive so that it is a win-win vs. a lose-lose incident.

DAVE:

Ronda, one of my issues is anger-management. I have learned depression is anger turned inside out, so occasionally my anger has been more explosive for the comfort of people I am with. The steps you just shared are going to be reviewed and practiced.

These days, the news is full of aberrations from normal human behavior. For example, this very morning I read online about a woman who was raped in prison by a transgender inmate. This person was a man who identified as a woman! And I assume the prison was obliged by law to accept this man's self-identification as a woman and house him in the woman's section of the prison.

RONDA:

So, I can imagine easily how angry this story made you. Now, tell me how you might apply my steps to this example. Remember, of course, as I teach in my book *Taming the Lion Within: 5 Steps from Anger to Peace*, that being angry at an injustice is not wrong unless it is disproportionate, and unforgiving or vengeful.

So now read again the steps I introduced earlier about bringing the issue to God and accepting His permissive will, and let me hear a free flow response of how these could help.

DAVE:

Ronda, when I read your first step, of bringing the issues at hand to God in prayer, I think of my grandmother. She described her reaction, with my grandfather, to losing three of their nine children in childbirth in the early years of her marriage. She said, "we just accepted these burdens together."

To accept God's permissive will about this trans-gender rape, I stop and ask myself, "why does God, who loves me so much, allow this abuse by this transgender person and the political apparatus supporting his self-identity."

Maybe I found an answer in the communion verse in Sunday's Traditional Latin Mass. Psalm 77, 29-30:

"They did eat, and were filled exceedingly, and the Lord gave them their desires … which they craved."

RONDA:

You mean, I suppose, that because God gave us free will, after the Fall, that could result, sometimes, in terrible decisions. Does that not remind us to love the sinner even when we hate the decision?

Now remember the second step:

Ask myself, "would I rather have robot 'yes-men' around me who automatically agree without a moment's conflict?"

DAVE:

This thought occurs to me, "what benefit is there if we just preach to the choir?" In my experience, we circulate our ideas with people who agree with us. I do this in e-mail or on Facebook. And when I make an exception and talk about those same ideas with family or friends who disagree, I irritate them.

RONDA:

Right! So, would we rather only have allies, and no family or no friends who are not allies?

Often, I find myself ready to scream at someone spouting culture of death ideas, or I want to nail them to the wall.

DAVE:

Isn't that your choleric nature, Ronda? We need more teachers to challenge our flawed ideas.

RONDA:

If I am angry enough about some issue, I sometimes go through whole hours imagining shunning for the rest of my life those beloved family and friends who disagree. But, then, of course, I realize that is disproportionate, unforgiving anger, and I pray for them and God gives me grace to forgive.

Circulating a draft of our book *Always a New Beginning!,* a family member of mine was stricken by the very idea. "But we love each other. How could you conceive of cutting any of us out of your life?"

I replied, "Well, I never have done so." Still, I wanted to try to explain how painful it is to differ with loved ones about issues that involve life and death. In some cases, it might be differing on whether one could vote for a pro-abortion candidate or, in others, someone thinking abortion wasn't even wrong.

DAVE:

Ronda, this is so insightful, especially in a big family like mine. But, you know, I've formed some habits over my sixty-eight years which I can't break easily.

Recently, I reacted to a Facebook post depicting two pro-abortion Democratic U.S. Representatives standing behind Speaker Nancy Pelosi. I immediately wrote a Facebook post of my own detailing my experience with faithful pro-life Democrats in Connecticut when I was in my early thirties.

I posted my angry reactive thoughts on my Facebook and e-mailed them to members of my family and Connecticut friends. I have stopped writing family members and friends if I know I might irritate them.

Ronda, I did not go back to read your steps. Of course, in this culture, we're not going to have everyone agree with us.

I guess it's time for me to have 'a new beginning.'

RONDA:

Let's look at my step three in this context:

Step 3: Thank you, Holy Spirit, that you have brought me to the truth about the matters being debated nowadays.

In the case of a dispute I was having with a family member, I realized how much of my ability to know the truth came from studying with wonderful Catholic philosophy professors. My relative, who disagrees about voting issues, never received that training. Couldn't I forgive her for being confused?

DAVE:

Ronda, my relatives and I grew up in a nominally or practicing Catholic environment rooted in old Irish loyalty to the Democrats. Because of my introduction to pro-life and traditional Latin Mass circles, my political attitudes changed when Ronald Reagan was President. My views would be considered by these relatives as "a road not travelled."

My thirty-three-year-old son, a generation removed from that Democrat and religious heritage, is teaching me to remember the world I live in, is much different from the reality he knows.

RONDA:

Yes, that's exactly what taking my step 3 is designed to help you think out. You may have arrived at the truth partly because of factors not in the lives of those who are disputing with you.

DAVE:

But, of course, they don't think that I have arrived at truth. They think they are right.

RONDA:

The purpose of this chapter is not to refute skepticism or relativism about truth, but only to see how to keep our reactions toward those who disagree from jumping, figuratively, grasshopper fashion, at their throats!

How much better if we quiet our judging minds before proceeding to further discussion.

Now, let's look at Step 4 in relationship to some experience of yours.

Step 4: Holy Spirit, tell me how to make this immediate issue online or in my head, after watching something on TV, into something positive so that it is a win-win vs. a lose-lose incident.

DAVE:

Ronda, I need to acquire this practice. My mentor when I lived in California, Fr. William Kiefer, taught me "we acquire the virtues through practice." I am still in need of much practice.

RONDA:

Okay, let's practice. Take the example of being outraged by the trans-gender rape. How could you turn that anger into something win-win?

DAVE:

Ronda, tell me if you think this makes sense.

The thought comes to me, David, slow down before responding. Slow! (Making a silent command to myself.) Allow for tension to move out of your body. Take a deep breath. And remember not everybody has the benefit of your formation.

RONDA:

When I slowed down, I thought, maybe God allowed this rape as a way to show what consequences could follow ignoring the way He created us male and female. So, next time I am talking to someone about how God created us male and female, I could bring in this shocking example to illustrate my points. That would be win-win instead of the lose-lose of ridiculing someone else's points of view.

DAVE:

I agree. I think people respond better if we don't talk down to their point of view.

For the Readers:

This chapter is pretty intense. We suggest you re-read it slowly thinking about examples of your own and applying the steps to them:

Step 1: Bring the issue to God in prayer.
Step 2: Do I only want to be with those who agree with me?
Step 3: Gratitude to all who have brought me to truth.
Step 4: Speak the truth with love to hope for a win-win vs. lose-lose.

5.

PRAYING FIRST VS. BLURTING OUT THOUGHTS

RONDA CHERVIN

"Know this, my beloved brothers: let every person be quick to hear, slow to speak, slow to anger; for the anger of man does not produce the righteousness of God." (James 1: 19-20)

RONDA:

I grew up in an atheistic home with Jewish ancestry. In our culture, most people talk a lot and interrupt all the time to get a word in edgewise! I can truly say that in eighty-two years of life I have never had a thought I didn't share in words with others!!!

DAVE:

My brothers and my sisters-in-law would say the same about me: he never had a thought he didn't share.

RONDA:

But you never rudely interrupt, Dave.

DAVE:

You're wrong. When I'm anxious, I often do rudely interrupt people.

RONDA:

Still in general, I find that I am different from those coming from most Christian families where children are taught to watch what they say and make sure it is good and loving!

So, when I became a Catholic at age twenty-one, I had to learn that there was such a thing as sins of the tongue and even that it was rude to interrupt.

Now, trying to "clean up my act" before leaving this world, I am working on a new beginning. It will involve at least a quick prayer to ask the Holy Spirit before I say anything about any important matter to anyone vs. blurting out whatever happens to be on my mind.

My first endeavor is to try to listen vs. interrupting. As one sage put it, some overly-talkative people are like drivers who have one foot on the brake but the other on the accelerator so that whenever there's a chance they can leap ahead of the other cars.

DAVE:

Exactly! And I also sometimes do drive that way. But now in my new beginning I remind myself 'slow' as I get into the car. And, picking up the theme of your first chapter, I tell myself be graceful not jerky.

RONDA:

So far, in the week I have been working on my new beginning, I have been trying to avoid just blurting out things in the form of interrupting others. I have learned a lot. Such as, often the words I wanted to blurt out were not relevant to the meaning behind someone's statement.

For example, during a gathering of a few friends, the hostess says "I'm a little tired. I'm going to take a nap. See you later." Before she gets to "see you later," I am interrupting with something like "But, first, listen to this story that you will be especially interested in."

"I'm not interested in your stories," the hostess replies rudely.

This wounding interchange would not have happened if I had not interrupted but, instead, said something like, "I'm sorry you're tired, have a good rest."

Dave, maybe you interrupt sometimes, but I don't notice that you interrupt a lot. Were you brought up to be polite and listen well?

DAVE:

Yes and no. I have to say that in the emotional turmoil of my upbringing I learned to suppress my feelings. So, as I have grown up, my tendency has been to be polite but for the wrong reasons, when seen from a psychological standpoint.

In recent years, I have tended to interrupt before listening carefully as I am preoccupied with making sure to express my thoughts. This results in awkward moments like the wounding interchange you described. I don't always have good boundaries.

With my therapist, I have learned over the years to practice mindfulness in the form of questioning my thoughts before expressing them. Your insights in this chapter reinforce this practice.

RONDA:

With respect to listening vs. blurting things out, one spiritual director asked me to watch to see how many sentences in a day of conversation start with the word 'I.'

I was ashamed to have to admit that most of my sentences begin with the word 'I.'

"So, what should I say, instead?" I asked.

"How about asking the other people around about their day, their thoughts, hopes, etc."

Now, clearly that would lead to listening instead of blurting out something about myself!

Trying to be less self-centered for a new beginning, I have found results to be surprising.

DAVE:

If you could only hear the advice my son has given me.

"Dad, ask questions so you listen to the other person. Then, you are not left anxious about something you said."

RONDA:

How different are these two conversations?

Blurted out the moment I see my friend: "So, I can't wait to tell you what happened to me since I last saw you!"

Or,

"I have been wondering what you have been thinking about our project. Can you tell me?"

A spiritual friend of mine, Louise Walkup, told me about a motivational writer who insists that if you don't first let the other person talk, they will not listen to what you have to say. Instead, they will only be waiting until you stop so they can tell you what they want to say. Lose-lose!

DAVE:

A form of this for me would be to remember to slow myself down enough to express interest in the very words a person has just said, instead of my own thoughts.

RONDA:

Let's see the role prayer can have in daily situations. A friend told me that something I did was not sanitary – it involved using a dirty old rag to wipe a sink. After apologizing, my first impulse was to blurt out everything this person does that I don't like. Instead, I prayed to forgive the person who had told me off, especially since he was right, and not to retaliate with examples about this person's habits.

Dave, are you able with God's grace, to pray for someone instead of paying them back in kind when they say something that hurts your feelings?

DAVE:

When I bump into people I know, sometimes even in an elevator, they often find an excuse to express their political or religious views opposite of mine. My son is teaching me to withhold my answer and just smile and be friendly. But sometimes I react impulsively. When I'm driving in my car nowadays, I'm trying to learn to slow down if I feel crowded on the road.

RONDA:

At our charismatic prayer group, I asked the members to pray over me to avoid blurting out things and to pray first for guidance of the Holy Spirit.

I have been doing better when I pray first. But, then, I noticed a very subtle form of interruption – that is letting my thoughts slide away from the words of Scripture and Liturgy at Mass to think about my own plans for the day.

Jesus seemed gently to chide me for interrupting Him by so doing.

DAVE:

Ronda, when I am in Church at parish meetings, I find myself raising my hand with questions. I am in need of guidance by the Holy Spirit. I tend to ask my questions as they come to mind, without thinking. Even though some participants compliment me on such questions, sometimes I think I ask too many.

RONDA:

I happened upon this exhortation in:

The Explanations of the Psalms by Saint Ambrose: Psalm 36
From Office of Readings, February 20

Open your lips, and let God's word be heard

"Meditate, then, at all times on the things of God, and speak the things of God, when you sit in your house. By house we can understand the Church, or the secret place within us, so that we are to speak within ourselves. Speak with prudence, so as to avoid falling into sin, as by excess of talking. You speak along the way if you speak in Christ, for Christ is the way. When you walk along the way, speak to yourself, speak to Christ. Hear him say to you: *I desire that in every place men should pray, lifting holy hands without anger or quarrelling.*"

DAVE:

Ronda, this reminds me of the concept from the retreat Manual *The Artist's Rule* we worked on last summer about the 'inner monk.' To envision speaking to Christ means, for me, to speak with reverence and probing thoughts.

But, my brother, Dan, embodied this point dramatically to me one night when I was visiting him in Maine. He was beating me bad at cribbage. Being over-tired, I lost my temper and screamed at him. Dan, who was physically fit and an imposing man, quietly clasped his hands in front of his chest, shut his eyes, and leaned slowly toward me.

My temper left me in a flash. There was silence for a moment. Then he looked at me with a measured eye – and said, 'let's resume our game.' Later, he told me that if he had not calmed himself down and had lost his temper we could have had a fist fight. And, he added, "Dave, you would have lost!"

RONDA:

I love that story, Dave. It strikes me as such a masculine exchange.

Here's a nice story of mine: I was at a restaurant in Hot Springs. The breakfast special included three slices of bacon. I remarked to the waiter that I was so poor growing up that I could never have more than one slice of bacon at a meal, and so three slices at his restaurant now made me feel that "I've arrived. I'm a millionaire!" The old waiter laughed. He said that as a child he was so poor that if he lost a mitten in the snow, his parents couldn't afford another pair of mittens, and he had to wear a sock instead.

The response of the waiter humbled me because obviously he had been poorer than I had been.

Concerning conversation, a question the philosopher Alice Von Hildebrand often asks me is this: "What is the theme in this present situation?" What she means is that if you enter the room of an ailing person in the bed, the theme would first be to sympathize, not to blurt out your latest ideas about something else.

A family member tells me that I speak too loudly. Since I am somewhat deaf, I sound soft when I am really being too loud. I beg people who are often around me to make a "ssshhh" gesture when I am too loud. Usually, they just give up.

"Guardian angel, please remind me to speak more softly!"

While working on *Always a New Beginning!*, I had a painful argument with a close friend. When I brought it to Jesus in prayer, He seemed to tell me:

"I am leading both of you away from so many words into My presence. So, words irritate you more easily at this time? That is how I detach you from them!"

I didn't take that to mean that I should be silent all the time, but given the plethora of words that flood my mind and I blurt off my tongue most of the day, I would certainly benefit from more silence.

P.S. Someone told me today that there is such a thing as an electro-magnetic personality. "Euphemism for choleric, rage-aholic, drama queen?" I asked. He said it was discovered that such magnetic personalities actually over-power the magnets in computers and can't even work with them!!!

For the Reader:

Perhaps you have no problem about blurting things out. Perhaps you always pray before speaking about anything sensitive or important. If so, God bless you. But, if you are like me, spend a week praying first and see if your conversations become more loving.

6.

WHAT TO DO
WHEN OUR QUIET LITTLE VOICE IS NAGGING
DAVID DOWD

"That when they shall see them, they may remember all the commandments of the Lord, and not follow their own thoughts going astray after diverse things, but rather be mindful of the precepts of the Lord may do them and be holy to their God." (Numbers 15:39-40)

DAVE:

I have a voice inside me that nags me. For example, I am often reminded of something I am supposed to be doing instead of what I am doing. Right now, a voice is reminding me ...There is a Pro-Life meeting going on in a local parish as I write this—should I stop writing and go to that? Other times, I can be nagged by a question like should I be taking a picture of the sunrise that I see from my balcony? These are distractions in my mind, competing for my attention.

I often find myself losing my focus, and this happens even when I am talking to someone.

RONDA:

Ah, well now, we have still another thing in common, Dave.

I find that since retiring, I have very little to do that is obligatory. As a result, I can go back and forth among three different tiny activities in my mind trying to decide which is more important and then do each of them badly.

DAVE:

Ronda, I this is where my daily plan helps. I have a morning routine. I have listed the tasks of my routine prior to breakfast and following that meal. Before I had such a plan written, I would get confused about what I was supposed to do next. I have found that in the three or four weeks since I wrote out the plan, my morning routine is much smoother and quicker.

RONDA:

What a good idea. I'll try it.

DAVE:

For example, our pastor in our local parish, Brian Campbell, a bright young Steubenville grad, ten and a half years ordained, just gave a workshop on Confession. He brought up a topic that I thought was relevant to me. He said, "Some of us can become nagged by every venial sin we commit. It is good to confess such things, but not to avoid receiving Holy Communion until we can get to Confession."

RONDA:

What helped me most with concern about going to daily Holy Communion, even if I had a venial sin on my conscience, was a teaching that we should not think of Holy Communion as a gold star for merit but rather as a remedy for sickness.

DAVE:

Some non-Catholic readers may not have the wonderful grace of the sacrament of reconciliation. But common to all of us are self-putdowns. We say to ourselves, 'you're not good enough,' or 'you can't do this now.'

Father also spoke of 'scrupulosity.'

Scrupulosity is defined as a "form of Obsessive Compulsive Disorder (OCD) involving religious or moral obsessions. Scrupulous individuals are overly concerned that something they thought or did might be a sin or other violation of religious or moral doctrine."

Father Brian offered, "if you have some form of this, you might start working on our relationship with God." We need to think of Confession as conversations with a God of love. We are to fear God in the sense of awe and in the realization that sin is real and so is punishment for sin. But not that He is a stern taskmaster just waiting to catch us in our wrongs. He is a forgiving Lord asking us to hold ourselves accountable.

RONDA:

I have often thought I was mildly OCD (obsessive compulsive disorder) and others certainly think I am overly-scrupulous. Pre-Vatican II, it was not considered scrupulous to debate about whether if, before Holy Mass, you bit your fingernail, which had food under it, you had broken the hour-ing fast before Communion and should, therefore, abstain from Holy Communion! Surely, nowadays, that would be considered the height of scrupulosity!

DAVE:

In so far as we have relaxed certain disciplines in the Church, I think we could question whether our self-discipline is as effective. Many people think there is no need for Confession because of missing Sunday Mass just to sleep in. Or, as many Catholics as non-Catholics, some say as many as 80% of Catholics in child-bearing years are committing the sin of contraception and never repenting of it.

RONDA:

Many readers may not understand why contraception is intrinsically wrong. Basically, fertility is a gift of God. Now, postponing the use of a gift is not wrong, as in keeping a bicycle given as a Christmas gift in the basement until the weather is better. But destroying a gift is wrong, as in breaking the bike in two out of pique.

Here's the analogy. It is not wrong to postpone pregnancy for serious reasons by avoiding sex at the fertile time of the woman's cycle.

This can be determined with great accuracy because of Natural Family Planning methods. But it is wrong to destroy the life-giving sperm or egg, or even worse, in the case of pills and I.U.D.'s, detaching the tiny but still human embryo from the woman's uterine wall.

DAVE:

This point struck me during an engaged encounter weekend. My then wife, Gail, and I were a couple on the team. When Natural Family Planning was being discussed, she brought the audience of twenty or thirty engaged couples to quick attention by her endorsement of the way NFP helped her understand and chart the way her body changes during her monthly cycles.

RONDA:

I hope some readers of *Always a New Beginning!* might actually read my book, "Making Loving Moral Decisions." (Originally entitled *Living in Love: About Christian Ethics.* It is now in print as part of the book *The Way of Love,* published by En Route Books and Media.)

Regarding OCD, I find it hard to pray quietly at home. That 'grasshopper' is always jumping to fix this little thing or that little thing such as straightening a picture on the wall that is slightly askew or a picking up a tiny piece of litter on the floor.

Then I scrupulously ask Jesus if He minds when I interrupt my prayers to fix these things!

DAVE:

I was wondering if I do this in my ordinary life? Yeah! Imagine I have to mop the floor or clean my apartment. I can distract myself from starting and procrastinate for twenty minutes before starting. Instead of thinking, wow, since God provided me this wonderful place to live, I need to be more aware and respectful in keeping my place cleaned up.

Instead of racing through tasks with a quick lick and a promise, I might think, "He gave me the time, as a retired person, to give some attention to this task."

RONDA:

Changing long-held habits is a long process. We can think, "Oh, I now understand all the reasons I do this foolish thing this unproductive way. So, I will never do it again." But that's unrealistic. Most likely we will try, fail, try, fail many times, but still get a little better at it.

But, Dave, does our scatteredness also impinge on daily relationships?

DAVID:

Yes. Don't we have many ordinary moments of encounter. For instance, in a passing moment with a clerk at Dunkin Donuts or Walmart, instead of perfunctory remarks about the weather, why don't I offer a kind word?

RONDA:

A Catholic evangelist I know, when in a restaurant with others praying grace before the meal, always asks the server, "And, what could we pray about for you?" Always the server is surprised and pleased. And, in some instances, this encounter has led to an on-going friendship.

DAVE:

At Church, I usually stay to pray after Mass. And by the time I leave the Church, most people have left. I am beginning to try to say a kind word to a couple of older men or a young family who might be gathered in the corridor outside the main Church.

I find that when I relate more lovingly to others, Fr. Brian's point makes more sense:

"God wants to form a relationship with us. He often speaks to us in our relationship with other people."

I thought of how many times I have felt stressed in social settings. I even had a practice of leaving conferences immediately after the speaker stopped talking, because, for me, the meeting was over.

RONDA:

(Laughing) You mean before the hens started cackling?

DAVE:

(Laughing) Maybe the desire to avoid the cackling was part of it, but I need to stop doing that.

But if I stick around, I might ask some of my fellow parishioners for their impressions of the talk. I might learn more than I ever anticipate from them!

RONDA:

And that cackling hen might just happen to be another Ronda Chervin. As a matter of fact, Dave, we renewed our acquaintance at just such an event!

DAVE:

I remember.

RONDA:

On sticking around after Church, by contrast, I am extremely gregarious and would find it hard to stay after Mass in my pew praying if it meant not getting in my little chat with some parishioner!

DAVE:

I want to circle back to my Obsessive Compulsive Disorder (OCD).

My son knows my OCD personality trait can get in my way. He knows my pattern of hyper-activity too well. But I feel blessed because he is an incredible, independent-minded man who cares deeply for his old dad. He sent me a poem, he wrote several weeks ago.

In his poem, he encouraged the reader to go for a walk in the woods. He encouraged the reader to suspend busy thinking. To just 'be.' And notice, in silence, our senses.

And notice what we saw, touched, tasted, heard, and even smelled. Then he encouraged some rest and reflection for a few moments.

When I practice this method of fleeing from nagging thoughts, I also like to think of people I know who are compassionate. I like to dwell on those images, and then step back into my walk.

RONDA:

You have taught me to enjoy more walks because of taking me with you on some strolls along the beach when we both lived in Connecticut. Freedom from nagging thoughts might also be something I could enjoy if I was less busy.

DAVE:

You need to give yourself permission to get off the treadmill.

When I think about my experience with this, I recall going for a walk on a path in Vitale Park in New York.

During our retreat this past summer, we were encouraged to be mindful of the time of day, our age, the season of the year, the vegetation, the little creatures busy storing food or the birds flying and roosting on trees or on the water. I remember, instead of being in my own intellectual mind, I was encouraged to be quiet, to let nature speak to me.

I think this was a profound moment for me. I actually felt some interior peace. My racing mind pulled over to the side of the road and stopped. I stopped and enjoyed the information my senses gathered, and if I stopped my racing mind, I could ask myself what is nature saying to me.

Ronda, do you remember this exercise.

RONDA:

Yes, I do.

DAVE:

Before I forget, with my OCD, I can catch my thoughts speeding up, trying to say too much in a conversation and talking too fast and/or connecting ideas only in my mind instead of connecting them verbally in such a way that the other person doesn't get confused.

For example, I was talking with some new friends recently. As I was introducing myself, my subjects jumped from years ago to the present and back to years ago. One of the new friends interrupted me and said, "You think like I do. You jump from subject to subject, but I can't see any logic in the flow of your thoughts. Your time-line is hard to follow."

I work with a therapist who has been so patient with teaching me to practice mindfulness. This means that when I catch my thinking getting confused, I stop. I try to recognize my error and calmly reset my thinking.

I am slowing my mind down to recognize I am in a moment where my thoughts are not right.

RONDA:

Sounds good. So, do you mean that mindfulness is an antidote not only to jumpy thoughts but also to nagging thoughts?

DAVE:

Yes. The jumpy thoughts and the nagging self-deprecatory thoughts probably started when I was a very young boy. When parents would fight, I would recoil in fear in my bedroom. And, as you can imagine, I developed this practice in the flight part of the fight or flight reaction. My brother went for the fight part and became a thorn in my father's side. By fleeing, my parents might notice my wounded reaction and respond to my vulnerability by listening to me and speaking to me with sympathy.

RONDA:

Recently I worked with a spiritual counselor on my anxiety. This became a co-authored book entitled *Avoiding Anxiety on the Road to Spiritual Joy*. My director, Albert E. Hughes, insisted that behind all anxiety is a bitter root judgment from childhood. For example, he thought his father didn't love him because he was ugly. So, as a result, a boy such as he might as a grown up always think that if anyone ignored him it was because he was ugly.

DAVE:

In another twist on parent/child relationships, my son recently brought to my attention that ours is backward. His observation is that I seem to seek approval from him instead of the other way around.

RONDA:

A typical role-reversal when parents age.

Getting back to your wounded flight reaction to your own mother, when you feel insecure in any situation you fly back and forth in your mind?

DAVE:

Right. This is an insight. Because I felt so insecure when my parents fought, I was alone in my bedroom as a youngster. Interesting to realize that years later I would still go back to that dark room, figuratively, whenever I felt insecure.

As I might dwell on my current situation, my thoughts would regress to the feelings of insecurity from the dark bedroom. Such a regression would leave me vulnerable to jumbled thoughts, nagging thoughts, and other rabbit holes I might go down.

So, isn't this a new beginning as I practice this new sense of mindfulness. When I feel insecure, I need to stop and notice. I could turn to our Blessed Mother and ask her to help calm my mind and bring my thoughts to roost.

In my Traditional Latin Mass circles, I have been become aware of an important factor. Older ways of praying such as the rosary or novenas draw our attention off ourselves into the hearts of Jesus, Mary, and Joseph. By contrast, some contemporary ways of thinking keep us stuck in our own psyches. However, if our own psyches are like quicksand that is not much help!

RONDA:

Good. Good.

DAVE:

And, of course, as I have aged, jumpy or fleeing thoughts can become more pronounced.

I might be sitting in a doctor's office and hear an unkind word and assume it was said about me. My behavior would change. The unkind word would trigger insecurity inside my head and, then, I couldn't concentrate if I was reading a book.

I can laugh now, but I have noticed human nature doesn't change from the playground at school to when we get older. In other words, when kids on the playground notice another one who is overly shy, what do they do? They pick on him, as a form of entertainment, to see what he might do in reaction.

Well, this can lead to buckets full of quicksand.

RONDA:

What do you mean? I get that you were miserably bullied. Does this relate to scrupulosity?

DAVE:

When the attention grew hurtful, I would hide behind a calm exterior, while under the surface I heard a voice telling me they are right. I can find myself becoming a little unhinged questioning everything I did or said for fear of being rejected.

Athletics had a big role in helping me grow out of this syndrome.

RONDA:

How?

DAVE:

When I was distance running in my late twenties and thirties, I would do my stretching before and after my run. I had some Runner's World stretches I would carefully follow. Slowly, I would follow the technique for each stretch. This slowed down my thinking.

Today, after my hip operations, I am doing stretches again. A new beginning! Sixty + stretches... from my neck to my toes!

I do stretches slowly, paying attention to my muscle and bone movement. This slows my thoughts down.

When I am driving in the car in traffic, I try to say...'slow'... to myself. My dad was a very patient driver, so I remind myself to be more patient.

Last night, I was in conversation. I over-reacted to a comment someone made. I caught myself and slowed myself down ... And I listened carefully to conversation for several minutes, without interrupting, until I felt my heart and mind stop racing.

For the Reader:

When does your nagging grasshopper mind leap around in a disjointed manner?

What can you say to yourself to calm down in such moments? Would small prayers help?

7.

WALKING VS. HUDDLING IN FRONT OF THE PC
RONDA CHERVIN

RONDA:

Context: I am an 83-year-old woman, in pretty good health, living in Arkansas with my granddaughter and family in a beautiful woodsy area by a lake in Hot Springs.

As a newly retired person, I have plenty of time to walk or do other physical exercise. Indeed, I have been urged on to such activities by every doctor or friend I have ever known! Nonetheless, I resist.

Here is my bumbling excuse...one you have probably never heard before: I identify with my soul: mind, emotions, and will. Not with my body!

DAVE:

Ronda, I am a 68-year-old male, living during the winter on the East coast of Florida near the ocean and beautiful natural parks and beaches. My brothers also live in Florida in the winter. My son and his wife live up north.

I am a newly retired person. But with high blood pressure and high blood sugar. So, I am motivated to exercise. I include in my daily routine walking, stretching, and core exercises.

These exercises do help me feel more in touch with my body, especially as I lose weight. But, with my emotional history, ups and downs throughout the years, I am not as in touch with my emotions.

RONDA:

There is a name for my way of thinking in Catholic spirituality. It is called 'angelism.' Angels don't have bodies. Some humans wish they were angels and didn't have the burden of having a physical component to themselves!

The good side is that we are less bogged down by bodily lusts than those who identify more with their bodily selves than their spiritual souls. Not, of course, that I don't like to eat or sleep or swim or to experience sex (when I was a married woman before becoming a widow). But even more, I love to think philosophically, to feel emotions of love, to exalt in plans I think I can make into realities. And my profession of teaching and writing requires lots of time at the PC on lesson plans and draft of books.

As a result, the idea that I need to walk more, do specific exercises, and move my muscles annoys me. It seems like a waste of time.

DAVE:

In 2014, after one of my hip surgeries, my step-mother, Cindy, said to me, "You've got to use them or you will lose them." She was referring to my hips, my legs, and my feet."

RONDA:

Well, I guess I need to listen to that advice! I surely don't want to be in a wheel chair for whatever is left of my life.

So, now I am being urged to make a new beginning by the fact that my feet are becoming numb for lack of circulation. From huddling over the PC most of my waking hours, my shoulders are slumped over. Worse still is a growing inertia such that the idea of even arising in the morning seems onerous instead of exciting.

Dave, do you identify with any of this?

DAVE:

Yes, my friend, I do.

Mostly, on the physical side, so let me respond to that part first.

My years of "desk labor" left me prone to pinched nerves from the neck through the shoulders. And my hip replacements, including three adjustments to my left hip and then a second total hip replacement, left me in poor shape from years of lack of exercise.

And my overeating during these years ballooned my weight to as much as 274 pounds!

In the past two winters, I first focused on daily swimming for one winter and then this winter on the routine of walking, stretching, and core exercises.

My weight this morning is 221 pounds!

I am also working with a great nutritionist. Phara J. Taylor, in Port St Lucie, FL, is working with me on Vegan fasts and detoxing!

The result is my blood sugar and blood pressure issues are resolving!

RONDA:

Oh, Dave, I have known you a good ten years, but I didn't know so much about all you have gone through. Maybe sometime in this dialogue you could tell me and the reader more about how you got through these terribly painful things.

Vegan fasts? I really don't know that much about vegetarianism. How strict is your diet now?

DAVE:

Ronda, my nutritionist has provided me with a step-by-step change in my eating habits. The changes in this new beginning for me were gradual. Now, I am enjoying preparing many ingredients for my salad including grilled chicken.

But getting back to my other challenges, pride, anger, and lust go on.

Being in Florida, it is an occasion of sin to walk on the street or beach! I have to practice guardianship of the eyes and mindfulness! My red blood can move a little quicker at times!

And the tough part is getting rid of images once they get lodged in my mind.

This might be why I connected, fast, with St. Benedict's saying, "Always, a new beginning." Because I certainly need a new beginning in this area. I don't want these bad thoughts dwelling in my mind.

And why I frequently say Hail Mary's during the day... asking for grace, 'now.'

I am making the Consecration to St Joseph during this season of Lent. In his book *Consecration to St. Joseph*, Fr. Donald Calloway, MIC, introduces St. Joseph in the most personal terms.

These help me see myself as a (divorced and annulled) husband and father enriched by new prospects for prayer and meditation.

But I still huddle with my iPhone too often.

RONDA:

What you just told me about will help me try to improve on exercise.

So, when we thought of dialoguing about New Beginnings, the idea of a chapter on walking vs. huddling over the PC seemed like a good stimulus to healthy change.

As I start this new beginning, here is my prayer:

Father God, You created me to be not an angel but a human person, a soul/body composite. I think of my twin-sister – so spiritual but using her body so creatively as a sacred dancer. Help me to try a new, better, way to move about day by day.

DAVE:

I love the way you talk with God when you pray.

After years of saying Our Fathers and Hail Mary's, I find myself trying to become more specific in the words composing my prayer. Sometimes, I feel silly. Like, is anyone listening? This is a new practice, so ... here goes!

Dear St. Joseph, wow, I've gotten much better acquainted with you doing the Consecration.

Your presence in the lives of your wife and son are so beautifully expressed! You walked so many times and to distant places!

RONDA:

Oh! I never thought about how St. Joseph has to be a model for walking...he went all the way from Bethlehem to Egypt and back, walking.

DAVE:

And, also, of course, he walked from Nazareth to Bethlehem for the census. Fr. Calloway notes that this was the first Eucharistic Procession with the Body, Blood, Soul, and Divinity of Jesus Christ hidden in Mary's womb.

In fact, Mother Angelica says, "Old men don't walk to Egypt."

Returning to my prayer to St. Joseph: "Can you help me with the 'trust' issue? I am a sinner and sometimes I am late for an appointment, and I can find myself driving like a crazy man to be on time."

"St. Joseph, you didn't even have clocks!"

"Can you help me, St. Joseph, acquire humility and learn to trust that being a few minutes late is ok?"

RONDA:

Here are some of my attempts to move about more instead of huddling in front of my PC:

- Taking Walks

- Housework

- 'Dancing' my Prayers

It happened that when I began this dialogue we had lots of cold and rain here, so the walks were sporadic and rather short.

Just the same, I found that the process of deciding to leave my PC, put on warm enough clothing, and walk through the door out onto the paths around our house and in the immediate neighborhood felt very good.

I love praising God the Creator as I watch little squirrels, ducks, and geese on the lake, and the sun-kissed waters of the lake.

Walking with my granddaughter, Jenny, and five year-old Teresa and one-and-a-half year-old Julia, in her stroller, to a little beach front near our house lifted my spirits. They walk twice as fast, but I didn't mind slowly making my way behind them at my own pace.

Whereas sitting at the PC, especially following national and church news, is depressing, walking in nature never is.

DAVE:

When my mind is whirling with the increasing pace of news pouring into my brain from the TV screen, I can get overwhelmed.

I live in a place where I can see beauty in the sunrise, in all the little creatures scurrying about, in gorgeous flowers, and in the variety of people.

Sometimes, I take my camera for my walk and post selected pictures on my Facebook page.

Pictures often get more attention than my other posts!

Do you want to tell me more about your second way of exercising.

RONDA:

Housework!

A short history of my life-long antipathy to such normal womanly activities is pathetic.

As a child, I avoided such required chores as making my bed, washing clothes, or helping with dishes with as many excuses as I could cook up.

Then, as a mother, these chores became inevitable responsibilities that could not be pushed aside.

The desire for order, characteristic of those of my "J" personality type (see Myers-Briggs Personality Types), kept me in a routine of housework. Still, I did my duty with reluctant grinding of teeth!

A humorous incident when my twins were three years old. During their nap time, I was lying on the living room couch reading the poems of Byron. My husband came in the door beaming with joy to present me with the gift of a better vacuum-cleaner.

"I hate you!" I screamed. Here I am immersed in ecstatic poetry, and you interrupt to present me with such a plebian machine!

A friend of mine, also a wife and mother, less prone to angelism, amazed me by this admonition: "Why, Ronda, how can you hate housework? Consider dusting and polishing a table reveals the beauty of the wood! Cooking is so creative!"

And, she added this to my shame: "How will your daughters learn to love their roles if you convey the idea that housework is a horrid burden?"

I did improve my attitude a little as a result of this happy home-maker-friend's hint.

However, now as a retired professional, living with my granddaughter's family, I find that laundry and dishes and cooking are pleasant ways of interrupting computer-i-tis!

It helps if I accompany such activities with prayers of thanksgiving:

"Thank you, God, that we have the resources to have clothing. Thank you, God, for the great variety of foods we can eat. Thank you, God, for water and dish-liquid, and pretty plates."

DAVE:

Ronda, your prayer reminds me to be more prayerful, myself.

During the ten years I lived in my little mobile home by the sea in Westbrook, CT, my "housework" turned into "no work" as I did my re-hab from a series of hip replacements and adjustments over the course of several years.

The good fellow who sold me the place built a beautiful wooden table in the galley kitchen.

Over time, my piled up incoming mail, magazines, bric-a-brac nearly rendered my desktop work/ printer area eligible for an episode of 'Where's Waldo?' (When my son was a youngster 'Where's Waldo?' was a popular series of books. Kids could try to find Waldo in elaborate settings.)

My brothers came in to get me back on my feet. Jim and his wife, Dawn, organized, pitched out, reorganized, and cleaned. My brother, Tim, came in and asked me the questions I should have been asking myself about what to throw out. My son spent a day with me in my shed. "Pitch, pitch, pitch" was our objective!

I remembered this was one of my Mom's favorite expressions: "Pitch, pitch, pitch."

As I got back on my feet, Dawn's comment, "See something, do something," gradually became my motto.

Now, I have three table tops that seem to gather stuff. But I follow a tip I learned on 'Minimalist Mom,' a Facebook group.

They recommend to periodically go through your house with a trash bag. Anything you have not touched in a month, ask yourself if you can pitch it out!

As a result, I am taking pride in keeping my place picked up! And, I periodically walk about with my trash bag in hand!

The benefits are less stress, less lost time, and fewer times I look, resigned, at a mess and forget to ask God to "Bless this mess!"

RONDA:

Bravo! I often tell participants in my classes and parish workshops,

"Heh, guys, the Church teaches that we should have simple life-styles. So, can we be living simply if we have so much stuff that we can't even find what we are looking for?"

DAVE:

I know a couple who will not even accept gifts. They don't allow anything in their house except what is necessary!

RONDA:

The attempt at a new beginning by more movement that I am enjoying the most is adding tiny movements to reciting prayers.

Praying the Our Father, seated, I lift up my hands above my head for the opening. "Thy kingdom come." I draw my hands toward me to illustrate something coming, and so on.

Now, my twin-sister, Carla De Sola, the sacred dancer, composes beautiful, elaborate dance prayers. You can google that name and see some of them.

But, simply adding tiny movements to my prayers adds a good element of the physical to the soulful.

At a prayer-meeting someone referenced the words from Zephaniah 3:14, "And the Father will dance as on a day of joy." I asked the leader to find on her iPhone the song to those words. Then, I jumped up and grabbed the hands of one after the other of the eight prayer-group friends and danced them around.

It felt so good to have our bodies join in our spiritual prayers. I found, also, that it removed a certain distance between us.

DAVE:

You call to mind the idea that we can make tiny judgments about others that can disappear when we are in movement together. You might be surprised, but I noticed this happening at the beginning of road-runs. Everybody stands around – people of all ages, both sexes, all shapes and sizes. But, when we start running together we glow like a school of fish in the sea.

Ronda, I just skimmed Carla de Sola's Wikipedia page. She is accomplished in her field of sacred dance!

Two thoughts strike me.

Men are interested in sports where the athlete's body is subjected to vigorous training (we say whipped into shape) and then entered into competition where, as they say, only the strongest survive.

Women, on the other hand, find elegance in movement in dance, ballet, horseback riding, and so on.

I have found myself trying to perform my duties more gracefully, Ronda, as we've been writing together.

Dare I say this is a "New Beginning" for me?

For the Reader:

Do you find yourself spending too much time huddled over your PC or other devices?

What kind of exercise might you try in the interest of better health?

8.

CHALLENGE OF CORONA,
ALSO A NEW BEGINNING
DAVID DOWD

"Who forgives all your iniquities: who heals all your diseases."
(Psalm 103:3)

(Note to reader: This is the first of two chapters about Corona. They were written originally in March, 2020, quite a bit before it became clear that this was not a passing problem but a major disaster. Since all readers are totally familiar with the enfolding of the Corona threat, when reviewing the manuscript for publication we decided not to update these chapters but leave them as they were written in March, 2020.)

DAVE:

Ronda, here we are, you in Arkansas and me in Florida, and we are in the middle of a national, world-wide, New Beginning!

The Challenge of Corona!

RONDA:

Now, David, it could be that this whole episode is but a memory by the time our readers have our book in their hands. Perhaps, should another episode of crisis occur, the need for a new beginning and spirit of charity will be useful.

DAVE:

At Mass this morning, the Feast of St. Joseph, at Holy Family Church in Port St. Lucie, Florida, Father Tri Pham had the regrettable task of announcing all public Masses in the Diocese of Palm Beach will be temporarily cancelled. He also reminded the parishioners, the Church will remain open with our Lord in the Tabernacle for prayer.

RONDA:

At the time of this writing no one in my family or friends has died of Corona. For myself, I am not afraid at all of dying of it. But, then, I am 82 years old, and that can make a difference.

For me, the most shocking part of this plague is that there is no Daily Mass in Church. I have been a daily communicant for some sixty years. I am watching the Mass on TV and making acts of spiritual communion.

DAVE:

I have also been watching TV Masses. For example, the traditional

Latin Mass from Limerick Ireland.

RONDA:

When watching TV Masses, because we are not receiving Holy Communion in church, we are prompted to say a prayer of Spiritual Communion. I particularly love this one:

O my Jesus, I prostrate myself at Your feet, and I offer You the repentance of my contrite heart; a heart humbled in its nothingness, a heart humbled in Your holy presence. I adore You in Your Sacrament of Charity, the ineffable Eucharist, and I desire to receive You into the poor dwelling of my heart.

O my Jesus, come to me, since I, for my part, am coming to You! May Your Love embrace my whole being, in life and in death. I believe in You, I hope in You, I love You. Amen. (Rafael Cardinal Merry del Val)

Tell me more about your Mass this morning.

DAVE:

Father Tri spoke with sorrow when he said the rectory has had calls from parishioners saying the local food stores, Publix, Winn Dixie, and other grocery stores, are out of meats and other food items.

Father's pastoral encouragement was immediate. He reminded us that this time during the Corona crisis can be used for family time. He compared our usual routine of rushing from work to sports practices to doctor appointments and to school with this time when we are asked to remain in our homes.

In further spiritual support, Father remarked: "St Joseph was a humble man. In addition to his role as protector and provider for Jesus and Mary, Joseph returned from sheltering his family in Egypt during the threat of King Herod to his ordinary tasks.

Today, some people seemed obsessed with gathering knowledge on social media instead of attending to their ordinary tasks.

I think of the fun my son and his wife enjoy in preparing fresh ingredients for meals. Then, I compared their pace of life with my "rush, rush, rush" to pour through Internet posts, newscasts, and the Facebook posts, my friends' posts...

Father reminded us to take the time for daily prayer, or living a virtuous life, and for being to present to members of our family...

RONDA:

I am noticing how my favorite priests are taking this opportunity even in homilies on YouTubes to drive home their favorite ideas of how we need to change.

DAVE:

The discussion of St. Joseph, in the *Consecration to St. Joseph* written by Father Donald Calloway, MIC, a Divine Mercy speaker and writer, popped into my mind...

St. Joseph was the person chosen by Almighty God to be provider and protector for His two most cherished creations...Mary, the mother of Jesus, and His Son, Jesus Christ. Joseph sacrificed his life, but he also spent his lifetime, as Fr. Calloway wrote, in "Eucharistic Adoration" of

Jesus. He also protected Jesus and Mary during the first "Eucharistic Processions."

Joseph protected "the Body, Soul, Blood and Divinity, the Miracle and Gift of the Most Holy Eucharist...walking from Nazareth to Egypt and back....and from Nazareth to Bethlehem, yearly, for the census, and back..."

RONDA:

What a fascinating image! I love it.

DAVE:

Father Tri suggested we gather together in our homes for prayer, not just for meals. And we use our together time, not to bicker and argue, but to pray.

Ronda, he suggested we use this time to become like monks in our own homes!

RONDA:

I like that suggestion from Father Tri. Most of my friends are going to Churches where even if there is no Mass for the public, they have Eucharistic Adoration. On the other hand, in some places they are being told that just staying at home is the only remedy. In that case, they are often watching Eucharistic Adoration YouTubes.

DAVE:

One pro-life priest I know, Fr. Frank Pavone, is providing Eucharistic Adoration, the Divine Mercy Chaplet, and the Rosary at Our Lady of Lourdes in the very Shrine of Our Lady of Lourdes in France during the Corona scare.

Even if when you read this book the Corona virus is long gone, you might love to click on Priests for Life, Abortion TV YouTube. You can access archives of past events.

RONDA:

Ah, very good advice. My situation is different. I am living in the lower suite of my granddaughter's rental house in Hot Springs, Arkansas. Because my granddaughter had a cold and a slight fever, during the very first days of the scare, she is anxious about my possibly catching it. So, I am not able to be with family for meals or to do my usual chores.

Instead, for at least three weeks, I am truly living like a contemplative nun.

DAVE:

Sounds like something you've always wanted to do! Ronda, this is a kind of social isolation that will take a toll on everybody, especially someone as social as you are.

RONDA:

Well, I once tried living in a Hermitage as a dedicated widow. I was a lay guest in a hermit-village. Never heard of a hermit village? You probably haven't. Most Catholics, when they think of hermits, are imagining a single individual in rags in the middle of a desert in Egypt!

DAVE:

True. But even in a hermitage you are living in a community of people.

RONDA:

Actually, at the same time as those sorts of hermits prayed in the desert, there were also little enclaves where monks lived in their own tiny huts around a chapel but only spoke to each other once a week.

DAVE:

"Ever ancient, ever new!"

RONDA:

Anyhow, a priest I knew had founded a hermit village with a few monks. He believed in inviting burnt-out activists for a year of contemplative prayer on his property.

I was thrilled to take this opportunity. After many amusing

incidents, he called me into his office and told me: "Ronda, you're not a contemplative at all. You're a highly active woman with contemplative graces."

DAVE:

Ronda, do you find that right now in Arkansas, do you find you can call on these contemplative graces?

RONDA:

Absolutely, but the newer graces will be part of one of the last chapters in this book. For now, I want to write about the immediate nun-ish aspects of my necessary quarantine.

I find it makes a difference that I don't expect visits from the five year-old or one-and-a-half-year-old great granddaughters. I miss their cute little selves around, but it is also peaceful not to think I have to put things high up they could get into, and so on.

It works for me to stand at the top of the stairs to ask my granddaughter or her husband about anything practical I need to figure out, but I miss the cheerful camaraderie of being together on rides to Church, library, or stores.

DAVE:

Ronda, but you can still hear the sound of children's voices and can see them playing outside in the garden.

Have you adapted your prayer life to your solitude?

RONDA:

During my time of deep quiet prayer, Jesus seemed to ask me a bit sorrowfully, "Ronda, don't you want to talk only to Me during this unusual time of seclusion?"

When I asked Jesus if He wanted to give me a hint as to why God allowed this plague, He seemed to answer that "Many people will come to God because of it."

DAVE:

Let me tell you about what I have been going through.

My summer residence is a mobile home in Pine Tree Park on Conesus Lake south of Rochester, NY.

One of my neighbors, Barb Klein, sent a thoughtful email in which she offered to make her special homemade soup and bring our neighbors in the park (there are many of us) to doctor's appointments if transportation is needed. She invited our responses.

Ronda, I sat down and started composing a few suggestions for a new Facebook page.

They included:

Many folks live here in Pine Tree Park because they know nature, moving slowly and almost imperceptibly, provides interesting glimpses of life:

Trees have needles, but they are dropped to make a soft forest floor. Of course, there is the rising sap, returning after winter hibernation.

But don't evidences of approaching spring provide us great topics for pictures and discussion?

I provided some ideas for my neighbors at Pine Tree Park.

I did post these ideas on Facebook.

RONDA:

I think your take is wonderful. Let me know if you get reports from your friend about how they are doing.

For the Reader:

Did reading this chapter remind you of any new beginnings during your experience of the Corona threat?

9.

RESPONDING VS. REACTING DRAMA QUEEN STYLE
Ronda Chervin

"Whoever is slow to anger has great understanding, but he who has a hasty temper exalts folly." (Proverbs 14:29)

RONDA:

Most readers, I believe, will be familiar with the term 'Drama Queen.' When I was a youngster back in the 40's before TV, we listened on the radio to daily shows called 'soap operas.'

The 'soap' part was because these serials about the dramas of life were usually sponsored by sellers of soap. They were called 'operas' because they were as full of emotional conflict as musical operas with heroines as fascinating as the leading female opera stars.

But I didn't hear the term 'drama queen' until many decades after. That name was for the heroines of TV serials always reacting with passionate emotion to the ups and downs of their lives.

Now, further along, in my own 60's, I started using the term 'drama queen' as an explanation of a certain type of anger – one with which I was extremely familiar because it was my own syndrome.

DAVE:

Maybe I can have a part in this drama. My part is usually when I express my anger or impatience with myself or another person. Typically, when I'm late for an appointment, stuck in traffic, or when I'm frustrated with technology.

RONDA:

What is being a drama queen like? Here is an example from my own daily doings:

> Tech coach: Now, Ronda, if you just click on that symbol on your computer…
>
> Ronda: 'Just' - I hate that word. Right! For you, a techie expert, it is 'just' a minute to get this horrible PC to do your will. But, for me, who used to be an expert typist on an old Remington, it has been a nightmare to deal with this new-fangled monster!

Notice, how a rather common frustration has become a huge drama!

Now, here is how I use such an example to help others with anger-management.

"If you think of yourself as the heroine of the drama of life, and others as secondary characters, or walk-ons, then you will be angry every single day. Why? Because others see themselves as the heroes and heroines and will refuse to simply say the lines or do the things you would assign to them."

So, instead of the drama queen scenario with the tech person described above, the reformed Ronda will respond in a good, loving way such as:

> Tech coach: Now, Ronda, if you just click on that symbol on your computer …
>
> Ronda: Thank you so much for trying to help me. One little problem. I don't really understand what you told me to do. Let me tell you what I am seeing on the screen …

DAVE:

My work on self-management equips me to critically evaluate incidents where I lose my temper. For example, if I am late for an appointment, I can use accusatory words to knock myself down, such as 'You S.O.B.!'

Just the other day, I realized the fight inside me among good and evil and the consequences. That voice accusing me of being an S.O.B., is not from a good place. So, my response to this self-criticism is just starting. With time to remind myself, I say, 'Slow down, Dave, you are a good person and you can manage,' and then I actually ignore the voice from the bad place.

Here is a technique my sister-in-law suggested. When the internal debate starts in her mind, she asks "Who is the speaker?" "Who is the witness?" And then she asks, "Which neighbor is complaining?" I love the idea because this helps me begin questioning and then sorting the thoughts in my head.

RONDA:

Yes, Dave. I am familiar with several fairly recent spiritual counseling methods. Deliverance Prayer, popularized by Lozano, teaches participants how to be mindful of what is going through their heads. We are supposed to rebuke any spirit that is negative. However, as lay people, we are not to say prayers that only exorcists can say.

To use your example, Dave, a counselor might ask when you first heard that term S.O.B.? and, eventually, try to persuade you that whenever that vulgarism comes to mind you pray: 'I rebuke the spirit of self-disgust and lay it at your feet, dear Jesus. Take it away.'

DAVE:

Yes, you know, what you just told me could lead me into a New Beginning!

RONDA:

So, back to my drama-queen idiosyncrasies, my challenge in working on this new beginning is to track day-by-day the impulse to react drama queen style vs. responding in a good spiritual way.

What is the spirituality of response, then, for me?

Probably what has now become a buzz word: responding vs. reacting.

For example, with being sequestered during the Corona epidemic, my immediate reaction was drama queen:

"I can't be alone downstairs! I hate being alone! I will lose my mind. I would rather die from contagion than lose my mind."

But going into quiet prayer my thought, instead, was more like:

"Hmmmm! Having more quiet time talking to Jesus could be peaceful. I could RESPOND more to whatever graces God might give me."

Praying deep breathing, looking out my window – that is a response to beauty vs. drama queen scenarios.

DAVE:

Ronda, this makes so much sense.

Let me explain. I have been accustomed to hustling through my day-by-day chores. I made myself a schedule, and I wrote down what I wanted to do step-by-step at the beginning of each new day.

For example, I make my bed and place my clothes for the day on it. Then I begin my bathroom routine.

This morning, I found myself slowly making my bed with a prayer of thanksgiving. The calm I felt and the neat and orderly way my bed looked was a real change.

The thought just occurred to me maybe we are 'big ships' (ha, ha), but our decisions to act out of our intelligence motivated by reason slowly change our behavior like the line on a tug boat slowly turns a big ship in the harbor.

RONDA:

Wonderful. You may not know, Dave, but after fifty-five years of teaching and writing I finally came up with a title for what I have been doing: A Phenomenological Exploration of Every Day Life!

DAVE:

Sounds like you've been reading John Paul II, I mean, John Paul the Great.

RONDA:

In case you don't happen to know what the word 'phenomenology' means, here is a very brief explanation. In the beginning of the 20th century, a German philosopher, Edmund Husserl, began to think in a new mode. Instead of writing about such realities as being, form, matter, change, etc., he decided to look at human experience and cull out the major themes that he found there.

But, whereas he and his disciples wrote about such big themes as time, eternity, and hope, when I started writing, teaching, and giving talks, I got interested in exploring much more minute realities such as how would your day improve if you thanked God even for toilet paper?

DAVE:

You mean that by studying with a great phenomenologist, Dietrich Von Hildebrand, besides teaching his insights, you veered off into such everyday life matters?

RONDA:

Praying quietly to Jesus about my drama queen tendencies, He seemed to say that seeing the drama in life is not what is bad. A dramatic understanding about elements of life is the literary talent God has given me. It is seeing myself as the heroine in an exaggerated way that is the bad thing.

I noticed that a benefit of my going to daily Holy Mass is that for a whole hour I am not the center of attention!

DAVE:

Your thought just stopped me in my tracks. So true for me, too.

This reminds me of the discerning of spirits of St. Ignatius of Loyola. One day, when I was in the beginning stages of my nutrition fast, my nutritionist provided me with two products. The products are a smoothie and a power green supplement. She provided me a schedule for a seven-day fast based on making my meals out of these two products. I would not have tried this without professional guidance.

In the midst of this program, I found myself very hungry, but ten miles from my house the thought came to my mind, like so many times before. I could have dropped in on McDonald's and grabbed a meal. Notice, this was a 'good' thought.

But, working with my nutritionist, I knew McDonald's food would have violated my fasting agreement.

But, discerning of spirits prepared me to see that this 'good' thought would actually lead to a bad outcome. I would have violated my nutrition fast. So, by discerning the spirit, I skipped the fast food and offered up my hunger for the remaining ten minutes and returned to my house where I enjoyed my nutritious meal.

RONDA:

On another topic, I remember a wonderful idea of a friend of mine who was a Catholic Hollywood actress. Mary Betten gave talks to Catholic groups. One of the challenges she gave that I found most helpful was this:

"Try playing the same scene you played as tragedy during the day and replaying it in the evening as comedy!!!"

To apply this maxim to my examples, couldn't I see it as comic that Ronda Chervin, Ph.D., professor and speaker, could be overwhelmed by so ordinary a thing as a PC!

Or, couldn't I laugh at the idea that a whole week or even a month of relative solitude during the Corona time would bring me to despair?

I wonder, David, could you tell me and the readers an example of over-reacting to something in your life which you could see, instead, as comic!

DAVE:

I am so serious-minded ninety percent of the time! Let me think. Though most men also curse other drivers in a traffic jam, why don't I slow down, take my foot off the accelerator, and chuckle at their frustration as they speed past me.

Ronda, I actually learned this practice from my brother, Dan.

But, I need to see the humor in situations that can frustrate me.

My brother Dan entertained people. Remembering him driving slowly on Route 91 North in Vermont in his AMC Pacer with his Irish cap on made me laugh. He was peaceful. I was so stressed.

RONDA:

Here is one of my most extraordinary examples of someone turning a real tragedy into something comic. There was a professor at our university whose name was Frank Sullivan. He was the most humorous teacher anyone would ever meet. For instance, on a sunny day when he knew his afternoon students would wish they could be outside instead of in the classroom, he broke them up by setting a ladder against the window of this first floor class room and entering by the window instead of the door!

So, Frank Sullivan was dying slowly of a blood disease. Everyone worried how his wife would do when he actually passed away. There we all were at the funeral. When we came up to her after the service to commiserate at her loss, she regaled us with this story: "The hospital called me in the middle of the night to tell me Frank had died. I heard a loud crack. The toilet seat broke in two just at that moment!"

DAVE:

I can see why Frank's wife would appeal to you. I think you have the same sense of humor.

When dear Jesus died, the walls of the temple cracked!

RONDA:

Exactly!

A good example of being a responder vs. a drama queen was a realization about my current vocation in life. I am used to being the center of attention as a professor or a speaker.

Nowadays, I am mostly retired from those roles. I am no longer the 'heroine.' However, as an acquisitions editor for the publishing house En Route Books and Media, I have lots of opportunity to use my God-given talents in helping newer writers with ideas about their books. I can suggest ways to improve a title or tell them why they need to describe their own lives more before leaping into their main themes.

I find this work very satisfying even if I am not the heroine, but a supporting player. I love helping new torch-bearers of the faith.

DAVE:

I want to say I hope you know you are the best mentor any person who wants to be a writer could ever hope to work with.

RONDA:

Oh, sure better even than Shakespeare, right?

Bishop Barron preaches that we want to see life as a theo-drama not an ego-drama!

Now here a really humorous example of a phony drama queen episode. It happens that my toilet stopped flushing properly a few weeks ago. It didn't help to try to pump it. Sometimes, it would work only after ten tries flushing it.

I was frustrated. Now comes Corona! I am quarantined to stay on my floor of my granddaughter's house, pretty far from the upstairs toilets.

"Aaargh! The toilet doesn't work! So, when it stops working, I have to clean up. Does my granddaughter and her husband want me coming up to their toilet in the middle of the night for my last "deposit?"

Happily, this drama queen reaction was resolved when the plumber replaced the 1940 toilet in our old rental house with a brand new one!

So, how could I have responded right away in a better more Christian manner, Dave?

DAVE:

This part I do want to hear!

RONDA:

Ronda: Jenny, dear. This is getting to be a problem. I try flushing my toilet but it takes many times to work, and it could get worse. What do you think is the best way to deal with this?

Jenny: It might take a few days before the plumber comes.

Ronda: Probably. I will offer this little cross up to God, and meanwhile, I am sorry if you might hear me going to your bathroom during the night.

Or, to replace "tragedy" with humor I could think: how funny to imagine me, a philosopher, cleaning up porta-potty.

DAVE:

(laugh) I cannot imagine Plato in a white suit in the local park cleaning a porta-potty!

But, how can we become so reasonable when inside an emotional tirade is going on?

RONDA:

That's a good question, and I hope by the end of this dialogue book we will have an answer.

Finally, I was moved when it seemed to me that Jesus was telling me that I would be less of a drama queen if I was more His bride. After all, brides are so happy to be with the bridegroom that they hardly get upset about trifles.

DAVE:

Actually, Ronda, I think me and our readers just encountered the philosopher in you.

For the Reader:

Are you sometimes a drama queen or a drama king? If so, what ideas in this dialogue could help you respond instead of reacting?

10.

CORONA RE-LOCATION
David Dowd

"But pray that your flight be not in the winter or on the sabbath."
(Matthew 24:20)

DAVE:

Greetings, Ronda. Here we are in New York State and Arkansas, each sheltering-in-place, practicing a social distance of some 1,500 miles, as we talk to each other on the phone. We are both old enough so that we remember that, when we were little, the very cost of a long-distance phone call would have been prohibitive.

I want to tell you about the next phase of my Corona Virus challenge.

RONDA:

Good. Like everyone else, I'm getting pretty rattled from all this time alone.

DAVE:

I can hear from the sound of your voice that you are rattled. I want you to calm down. Why don't we start with a prayer?

"Dear Lord, we are gathered here together in the midst of this shelter-in-place demand by the Corona Virus threat. Our anxieties from sheltering-in-place are beginning to be felt. We ask Your blessing, Lord, and Your peace to guide us each day as we work together on *Always a New Beginning!*

But we need to remind ourselves, God, Your love for us never changes. Ronda and I are social beings, and so often we obtain real support in the interactions we have with others. But, under the circumstances of sheltering-in-place, particularly in this season of Lent, we have to give up the benefits of face-to-face interaction with our friends.

Dear Lord, You remind us that Your grace is sufficient. In our anxious moments, please prompt us in humility to turn and receive Your grace in our hearts where we can be calm, peaceful, and purposeful as we seek deeper immersion in this New Beginning in relationship with You. We ask this through the grace of Your Blessed Mother and the grace of Your presence in our lives.

RONDA:

What a beautiful prayer! Thank you.

Missing so many face-to-face encounters, I did enjoy seeing some of my favorite priests living at a distance from me at their live-streaming Masses.

I was also thrilled to learn that, in some places, the abortion clinics have been shut down where babies are chopped to pieces in their mother's wombs.

DAVE:

Ronda, in days after the Coronavirus pandemic triggered national reactions, social media provided selected, rational, insightful guides.

RONDA:

Do you have any examples?

DAVE:

Yes. The following was posted by a Franciscan Capuchin Brother Patrick McSherry:

"And suddenly we woke up one day and everything had changed:
at Disney - the magic was gone;
the Great Wall of China was not so strong;
New York now sleeps;
and no road wants to lead to Rome.

A virus is crowned as owner of the world and
 we realize our fragility;
we do not know if the damage is on purpose
 or a result of our own irresponsibility,
but the roosted threat is there, and

getting stronger every day.

Memes aren't quite so funny anymore;
hugs and kisses have become dangerous weapons,
and the shortage of products on store shelves
shows us once again how selfish we are,
so selfish that we say, no problem,
this virus only kills old people;
as if we did not have parents and grandparents,
or as if we were never going to get there.

We want to assert our right to decide
 whether or not to let someone else live,
and now we realize that we cannot even decide
 our own destiny.

Our planet today puts on a mask not only
against a virus but to cover our vulnerability
mixed with pride,
and we wash our hands so as not to acknowledge
our responsibility, just like Pilate.

Yes, there is fear.
Yes, there is isolation.
Yes, there is panic buying.
Yes, there is illness.
Yes, there is even death…

They say that after a few weeks of silence,
the sky - blue and bright –
is no longer full of smog.
They say that in the empty streets of Assisi,
people are singing from their houses
and their balconies, keeping their windows
open so that those who are alone can hear
the voices of the families around them.

They say a hotel in the west of Ireland
offers free meals and home deliveries.

Today, a young woman I know is busy
handing out flyers in her neighborhood
that has her phone number so that
the elderly can have someone to call.

Today churches, synagogues, mosques, and
temples are preparing to welcome
and protect the homeless, sick, and tired.

All over the world, people are slowing down and reflecting.

Throughout the world, people see their neighbors in a new way.

All over the world, people are waking up
to a new reality. How great we really are.
How little control we really have,

and to the thing that really matters ... LOVE.

So, we pray and remember,

Yes, there is fear ... but there must be no hatred.

Yes, there is isolation ... but there does not have to be solitude.

Yes, there is panic buying ... but there doesn't have to be selfishness.

Yes, there is disease ... but it must not infect our soul.

Yes, there is even death ... but there can always be a rebirth of love.

Wake up today choosing how to live.

Today, breathe, pause, and listen behind the torments of your fear.

The birds sing again, the sky is clearing,
spring is coming, and we are always surrounded by love.

Open the windows of your soul, and even if
you can't step into the empty street ...

Sing."

RONDA:

I am reading many of these marvelous things people all over the world are writing to give others a perspective, but this is the most beautiful so far.

So, meanwhile, you are in Florida for the winter, but since you live most of the time in Rochester, New York, didn't you start thinking maybe you needed to go back?

DAVE:

Yes! As a matter of fact, on March 19th I was talking with a banker I know and she said that there are so many variables in the financial world impacted by the slow-down in the economy, we could face a financial collapse.

So, remembering my Grandmother said in her household, we always made family decisions together ... I wrote to my son and my brothers to relate this news.

I also mentioned to my family that Canada had closed its borders. And my friends from Holyoke, Massachusetts, who wintered in Florida, were packing up, to go back immediately.

I learned the Governor of Florida might be going to follow California, New York, New Jersey and Connecticut and issue Shelter-in-Place orders.

RONDA:

So, what did your family think?

DAVE:

My son and his wife discussed the matter. So, when I spoke with them later on March 19, they recommended I return to Rochester, New York, immediately.

So, I packed 13 boxes on the 19th and sent them by UPS on the 20th. I had my car serviced and learned I needed four new tires. So, I purchased and had them installed on the 20th.

RONDA:

That must have been pretty tense. Did you feel you got special graces to get through it all?

DAVE:

That's a good question. Since I had just made my profession to St. Joseph, he was with me, I believe, because the tasks I needed complete flowed smoothly. So, I think I did feel graces.

By the time I went to sleep on March 20, I was packed and ready to move back to Rochester, near my son.

RONDA:

St. Joseph moved pretty quickly, didn't he?

Dave, since I only needed to shelter-in-place in the lower floor of my granddaughter's house, where I have been living for a year and half, this whole problem of the Corona Virus threat has been much,

much, less dramatic.

But I am guessing that many of our readers, perhaps a year or more from now, reading your dramatic turn of events will bring back many memories of their own.

DAVE:

I must admit that I felt St. Joseph's presence in this move. A New Beginning!

On March 21, I was on the road from Hutchinson Island/Fort Pierce in Florida.

I drove 535 miles and stayed at a Quality Inn in Florence, SC, and slept well. I was tired!

My son called me before I went to sleep!

I was so gratified that Dave and Gwen shopped so that my cupboards will be stocked when I arrive at my cottage.

Then, dear Mary, my niece, checked in. She asked if I wiped my room in the Quality Inn.

I said, "Yes, and the Quality Inn front desk had said they were being real careful and put my worries to rest, but I still cleaned surfaces in my room myself!"

As tired as I suddenly felt, for my niece to check in, also brought me real comfort.

My carpenter in Livonia, NY, called. Mike is sprucing up and preparing my house for occupancy!

I relaxed, fast, as their kindness registered. I realized how tired I felt.

RONDA:

We spoke together on the phone while you were driving up North.

DAVE:

Just hearing your voice and discussing our work provided a sense of normalcy to my day!

RONDA:

I understand. Everyone has been talking about how discombobulating it is for people to be outside their usual routine. And, even though my Catholic commentators I read on the webs admonish us to use this time for more prayer, we still do feel those little tremors of "I don't know why I feel so jumpy?"

DAVE:

The reality we know from our past has changed. Our new reality is not familiar.

For myself, this means extra thinking as I proceed during the day. 'Not knowing' makes me jumpy. Techie stuff makes me jumpy because I don't know technology well.

But, Ronda, I wonder if that has to do with why you are jumpy. Think about how you don't have the social contact you are used to, so there is more stress.

RONDA:

Of course! My big techie helper, my granddaughter, has me on semi-quarantine, so I can't bug her every time there's a glitch.

DAVE:

So, a new day begins. I made note in my head 535 miles down and 770 miles to go!

Day 2, March 22, found me fresh and prepared to resume my drive, north.

Germantown, Maryland, became my destination. I wanted to avoid Washington, DC, traffic.

I arrived at the Holiday Inn Express in Germantown and checked in. My weary arms struggled, but I reached my room, ate dinner, and took advantage of the washer dryer on my flour to do my laundry.

Slept fast and woke up to an urgency to return fast. I watched the news on TV briefly. Could events in Washington impact my arrival in New York State?

I was going to get on the road and not take any chances!

Of course, I did my stretching and enjoyed a cup of coffee and a hard-boiled egg before returning to life on the road!

RONDA:

You know, Dave, I realize most men are leery of admitting to fear of any type, but, of course, I was praying for you on the road, imagining that you must be fearful given all the rumors of shut downs of businesses, schools, and restaurants.

DAVE:

Good point, Ronda. In my life, I've have had to deal with issues of fear. But, surprisingly, my mind-set during this re-location, possibly due to graces from your prayers and my Consecration to St. Joseph, was to maintain momentum, and I didn't pay much attention to the news.

RONDA:

Hurrah! A New Beginning.

DAVE:

Right! So, I got into my car, on March 23 and, I thought to myself, tonight I will be sleeping in my own bed!

Just 317 miles to Livonia, NY!

Moving north, the weather changed. Dramatically!

Sunshine and blue skies in Florida were long gone!

Ha! Ha! I was blitzed by SNOW SQUALLS as I drove through Southern Pennsylvania!

I stopped to admire nature's gift of falling snow. A light powder was blowing every which way in the wind.

During my break from driving, my pre-made tossed salad was delicious. I wrote thank you notes to people who have been supporting me.

RONDA:

By the way, dear friend, I bet that trip was pretty expensive.

DAVE:

My fast journey to return to New York was not cheap!

But I decided debt is a small price to pay for safe and sound near my son and daughter-in-law and in my own home.

Here is my budget for my relocation costs:

Travel from Fort Pierce to Livonia, NY

March 20

Mail 13 Boxes UPS.	$467.00
Oil Change & 4 Tires.	$870.00

March 21 From Fort Pierce to Florence, SC

Fuel.	$75.00
Quality Inn in Florence, SC.	$90.00
Food.	$10.00

March 22 From Florence SC to Germantown, MD

Fuel.	$75.00
Holiday Inn in Germantown, MD.	$119.00

Food. $10.00

March 23 From Germantown to Livonia, NY

Fuel. $50
Food. Dave & Gwen. $337

Total: $2,103

RONDA:

Wow! I sure am glad I didn't have to re-locate on my small social security and pension.

DAVE:

You're someone I know counts her blessings.

I arrived in Rochester to let my son and his wife know I arrived safely. I noticed the streets were near deserted as I drove into their neighborhood.

I called my son. He greeted me on the phone. He met me in his driveway but was immediately very clear with me.

"Dad, we have a NEW NORMAL!"

"Wash your hands. Physical distance of six feet. No spontaneous showing up at people's houses, and shelter-in-place."

The authoritative note in his voice struck me. He and my daughter-in-law would not even accept cash to reimburse them for the groceries. (I thought cash on hand might be helpful. They said no, we don't want cash from who knows where in our house! Please send us a check!)

Wow, my daughter-in-law's clear point in support of Dave's instructional tone left me pondering as I drove home. I thought to myself, Dad was learning "direct is more effective" for the New Beginning in our new normal in New York.

Another new beginning: the realization registered that my son and his wife were adults speaking to me in 'tough love.'

I returned to my cottage. My son called me once I was settled. I took notes as he repeated the key points from our earlier verbal conversation in his driveway.

Here they are:

Thank you!

NEW NORMAL SCHEDULE

New Normal YouTubes listened to – CHECK
Hands Washed - CHECK
Counters wiped – CHECK
Deck Swept - CHECK
Showered, Bed Made, Breakfast- CHECK

SCHEDULE To Do List

RONDA:

I also have found that keeping a list of my new at home schedule is helpful.

Mine goes this way:

Arise (no alarm now)
Morning Prayer
Breakfast
TV live streaming Holy Mass
Quiet Prayer
Work on Projects
Nap
Lunch
Walk
More work on projects
Dinner brought down by my son-in-law
Liturgy of the Hours
Reading fiction
Going to sleep

All these items interrupted by family video chats, Scrabble games online with a daughter, and lots and lots of phone-calls.

DAVE:

Ronda, because I have traveled up the coast, I am instructed to shelter in place fourteen days. Twelve more days as I write this!

And I have a new wild pet. A robin has been attacking my kitchen window. I have learned the robin sees his reflection in the window and is being territorial. This morning the robin exerted so much energy flying into my window, there were streaks and streaks of blood on the window.

I placed sunflower seeds around the trunk of the tree he roosted in. And I washed the window with a broom and an old washcloth.

I disposed of the washcloth and came in the house and washed my hands.

RONDA:

In addition to my daily schedule, I am finding that many things I did in a jerky vs. graceful manner, I now do slowly and more contemplatively. I look out my window at the lake sometimes for a good fifteen minutes.

DAVE:

Your reminder to consciously be purposeful and thankful, is helping me. When I woke up this morning after eight hours of sleep, I said my prayers.

Slowly and purposefully I made my bed. Mindful of your suggestion to be thankful, I washed my skin, our largest organ, bigger than the heart or the brain, carefully!

I might add that our Traditional Latin Mass parish in Rochester is live-streaming Holy Mass on Sunday at our regular time. Fourteen of us tuned in. Father Bonsignore will hear confessions on Palm Sunday.

Fr. Pavone, founder of Priests for Life, is celebrating an online daily Mass during this crisis.

RONDA:

As mentioned before in the first chapter on Corona, we wrote this early on in the crisis. Certainly, we agonized later with those reported to have suffered deaths in the family and heavy economic trauma.

DAVE:

Sometimes these struggles in one form of another strike close to home though not involving death or disease.

My niece, Mary, and her husband, Nick, are parents to three darling young daughters. Her husband works in a butcher shop. He is considered an essential worker. So, every day he goes to work and comes home and has to change his clothes outside the house and then shower before he can greet his children whom he adores.

For his trouble and risks, his company gave him an $80 bonus in his pay check. My niece who agonizes daily with the risk to her beloved husband, herself, and her children felt an injustice in the compensation her husband received for the risk he was taking.

Can you imagine the struggle and sufferings of the medical workers who sacrifice themselves daily in this trauma and intensive care units where people with Corona virus receive medical attention?

RONDA:

I am in admiration of my grandson's wife, Veronica, a nurse who is taking just such risks.

For the Reader:

As you recall your time during the Corona Virus Threat, what were the challenges, physical, economic, or spiritual?

Did you sense it was a call to *A New Beginning*?

11.

BEING LOVING VS.
TRYING TO CONTROL THE FAMILY I
Ronda Chervin and David Dowd

"Be completely humble and gentle; be patient, bearing with one another in love." (Ephesians 4:2)

(Note to Reader: The theme of family is so much a part of new beginnings that we found our text and photos began to mount to almost 30 pages instead of the usual 10 pages per chapter. I, Ronda, thought the easiest way to deal with this was to slice the original chapter into Part I, Part II, and Part III.)

(Second note to the reader: we have come to understand in new beginnings we become more introspective when examine our pasts. This is why this chapter is so much longer than the others. Also because of the many photos we inserted.)

RONDA:

For those of you not familiar with the story of my life, you need to know a little more to understand this challenge of a New Beginning. (You might like to read my autobiography entitled *En Route to*

Eternity, published by Miriam Press.)

I came from an atheist family where my parents were in a common-law sort of partnership.

My father left us when my twin sister and I were eight years old. After that, we saw him only on Sundays.

Even though my mother, twin-sister, and I were extremely close, I picked up from my mother the idea that friendship was more important than family.

Because friends were self-chosen, perhaps?

My mother, an editor, loved books and passed on that love to us. I recall being very surprised, when I became a Catholic at age twenty-one, to find that my new philosophers and writer friends actually thought that the birth of a new baby in our circle was more important than the publication of one of their books!

I married a book salesman, who was also a writer. But he, coming from an orthodox Jewish background, absolutely thought that family was the highest value. That was his belief even though he had become an atheist in his teens. He converted to the Catholic faith, after our marriage, many years later.

I expected to put family first when I became a married woman and, shortly afterwards, the mother of twins.

Unusual circumstances, however, somewhat skewed that expectation. After the twins came many miscarriages. At the same time, Martin, my husband, became disabled with severe asthma. I finished my Ph.D. in philosophy and became the full-time bread-winner of the family.

So many hours put into teaching, preparing classes, and marking papers gave me a dual identity – family/career.

As well, I was a zealous convert to the Catholic faith, a daily communicant, a charismatic speaker, and a writer of Catholic books. This gave me an identity in the Church different from that of most family women.

DAVE:

Our Family "Blood Line"

My mom and dad were sweethearts in high school. They came from very sports-minded, hard-working Irish families with traditional Irish Catholic upbringing.

When my dad returned from serving in WWII, as a Tech Sergeant specializing in French-English intelligence work, he married my mom who worked for American Airlines during the war. Dad went to work in the family insurance agency with his father. His grandfather had founded the agency.

Our Family Manger

In 1948 my brother, Jim, arrived. Then, in 1951, I arrived. Dan arrived in 1953, and Tim arrived in 1956.

Dad's mom and dad were very active in College of Holy Cross

circles and College of New Rochelle, New York, circles. My grandmother founded a Catholic Lending Library. In the beginning, she paid $25 a month rent to my grandfather. Business flourished as lay people become interested in the writings of authors my grandmother's library introduced.

Then, in 1960, Bishop Christopher J. Weldon, Bishop of Springfield, MA, supported the library with a donation of $2,500 - one hundred dollars for each of the 25 years the library had been open.

This allowed my grandmother to re-locate. The new enterprise became known as the Open Window Book and Gift Shop. The Open Window hosted annual book fairs, attracting such well-known authors as Archbishop Fulton Sheen, Tom Dooley, and others.

Dad's father was prominent in Holy Cross and Boston sports circles. He had been a star athlete in basketball and baseball in college so, as kids, we met Celtic and Red Sox players when they came to Holyoke. They were friends of the family and meeting them was fun! But family celebrations and family losses were part of our family. One of my sorrows in coming from a broken family is the fact that my son did not know his grandmother's family and heritage.

My mother's brother, Ed, retired, second in command of the Massachusetts State Police, and her brother, Bob, followed a career as a high school football coach in Whitman, MA, with service to the New England Patriots as a scout.

Gathering with the Teahan families at Thanksgiving or Christmas or on Cape Cod was always fun.

My love for our faith grew naturally from within the dynamics of Catholic enterprise and interest in sports happening in my little world.

Some may be surprised at the benefits one might find in sports activities. One learns discipline, regular exercise, and respect for the authority of experienced players and coaches. Ronda, do you see the way this might provide Catholics insight into the authority of their parents and their parish priests.

My son, Dave, studying the place where his great grandmother, her family, including his grandmother and uncle, are buried.

RONDA:

Yes. One of my sons-in-law is a baseball coach for teams his grandson plays in. Going to these games gave me a good sense of how fatherly the coach can be.

However, on authority in the Church, readers might be interested in a book I recently wrote called *The Crisis in the Church.*

DAVE:

Getting back to my story, as special as members of my family were, there would be setbacks, as with every family.

I suffered a couple of concussions as a kid. So, I emerged kind of shy and had a speech impediment.

Another issue, being strong-willed Irish, my parents would battle over differences. Neither the battles or the issues were understandable for me as a youngster. All I felt was fear.

These were important parts of my background, early sufferings which would be used to mold me into the person who would face the next several years not quite as sure of himself as his brothers were as sure of themselves. (At least as they appeared to me.)

RONDA:

The theme of this chapter, loving family vs. trying to control family, will be different for each of us and for each of our readers. Each of us is formed by our own experiences. So, I never heard my parents fight. But after my father left, a friend remarked, "Don't you think your children heard the silence!"

DAVE:

Your comment on silence speaks volumes to me. Silence is felt.

Tell me more about your family background.

RONDA:

Before you understand the idea of a new beginning for me now, I want to write about problems with controlling others in relation to my family background.

My mother was a rationalist. She despised tradition and considered enforcing behavior on one's children to be a throw-back to the past. She happened to work for quite a while as an assistant to psychologists. This increased her tendency to want to parent through reason vs. tradition.

When laying down necessary rules for us children, she would always explain the why of the rule.

For example, never: "come home right after school or you will be punished." Instead: "come home right after school because otherwise I could be afraid you were in trouble."

It is said that twins are a gang of two. My little girl twins certainly exhibited that humorous description. From earliest childhood they would do what they felt like with each other's support. Meanwhile, for instance, while they had fun throwing unwanted parts of their meals from their high chairs to the floor, I would be sitting miserably trying to figure out if manners were moral absolutes or only conventions. And, if only conventions, then how could I punish my twinsies for throwing around unwanted left-overs?

Dave, were you controlled a lot as a child and how did you bring up your son?

DAVE:

I don't think I was controlled. I am still good friends with Don Purcell, my neighbor and close friend growing up in Holyoke, Massachusetts. He and I still claim we had the best of everything as kids. We had a river, a reservoir, a mountain, a golf course and baseball diamonds within walking distance.

Don and Dave

We had friends to play with. Gary Proulx and I are still close. We played sports, went hunting and fishing together. And, surprise, even got in trouble together!

But beneath the surface, there were storm clouds gathering.

My parent's bedroom was in the center of a second-floor hallway.

My brother, Jim, had the big bedroom across the hall. My brother, Tim, was at the top of the hallway. Dan and I had our own rooms at the bottom of the hallway.

So, the battles my parents would have late at night were no secret.

In addition, often when I came home from school, my mom would be sitting on the couch in the living room by herself.

Sometimes, she would have had a drink or more. As a little boy, looking at her, I clearly felt her pain. We, as a family, would plead with her to stop drinking. But she was sinking into despair. We would later learn my mom might have been bi-polar, but in those days, we had no clue. She deteriorated in health as we progressed through junior high school.

So, the issue with me was not control. The issue was fear. Fear my world was crumbling and the two people I loved most could not prevent what was happening.

RONDA:

If you had led the writing of this chapter, Dave, you might have called it Fear as a Component of Control in Family. It seems to me it was only in the last few decades that psychological counselors started talking about how people become anxious whenever they feel they cannot control others.

I ask myself now, more than fifty years after I couldn't figure out how to control my two-year-old twins, what did I ever control?

Well, of course, I controlled basic daily matters such as preparing food, getting into bed at night. Most of all, however, I could control a classroom - enforce what the students needed to do to pass my courses.

I could also be sure that I could get to Daily Holy Mass.

I certainly couldn't control the family! In case one of them reads this book someday, I am NOT making a list of things they did that I didn't want them to do but they did anyhow.

DAVE:

Typical kids, if you ask me.

Mom and Dad took us to Church on Sundays as we were growing up. We did not think of it as control, just our Sunday obligation. School and homework were expected. My dad would check our report cards, and mom would have lunch made for us when we came home at noon.

We sure misbehaved. 'Wait until your father gets home,' were mom's words when we pushed the boundary too far. But mom kept a poem her brother Bob kept in his football team locker room on the bulletin board in our kitchen. 'Don't Quit!'

The control in our household was emotional control from the drama being played out between my parents and, for me, from my own stuttering problem and shyness.

RONDA:

I never heard you stutter, Dave?

DAVE:

I stopped stuttering in Junior High School. I met a Dr. Evvat. He recognized I had a cluttering problem, not a stuttering problem. He taught me to make a chart of how I formed every letter of the alphabet. Then, when I would run into a block, stammer on a word, I trained myself to remember the steps to form the first letter or sound and stretch my block. Eventually, my stammer disappeared.

Getting back to the question of control. I don't think I ever sought to control my son, David. If anything, I played sports with him, played soldiers, or went with him to the playground and encouraged him to find his own fun. I think I only spanked him once, as a little boy, but that was out of my own frustration with my own stuff at the time, as I remember.

RONDA:

How interesting! Continuing with my reflections, the fact that my twins were so hard to control doesn't mean that even now I don't try to control the members of my family. As of this date, excluding real but not to be seen until heaven miscarried babies, they consist of my twin-sister, three adult children (one who died), seven grandchildren, and four great-grandchildren. Also, of course, the husband of my sister, and husbands of children, and grandchildren. And, of course, my husband, who I assume has reached heaven by now – he left this earth some twenty-five years ago.

Mostly, I try to make family think the way I do, especially about the Church. Then comes trying to force them to do whatever I think would make them happy or would enhance my own life in some way, such as why don't we all move into an old house somewhere warm, like Florida, so we can all be together.

The concept of 'force' left me with questions. How do I force them? With what kind of threats?

Never physical threats since I am probably the smallest of all except for my twin and great grandchildren.

Nonetheless, everyone in the family would certainly say I was domineering.

I try to coerce them by yelling at them, or, of all things, logic!

"Don't you see that…"

And, occasionally, if rarely, with the thought of hell.

I have come to realize how 'drama queen' domineering it is when I yell at other people.

Here is a photo of my twins.

Last photo of my husband, Martin, just before he left this earth.

DAVE:

Ronda, I think I see something that has been missing in my life. I am not sure if this is good or bad, but starting with my grandmothers, who provided loving, Catholic examples, I don't recall being talked into going to Church.

I do recall my Mom took my brothers and me to Mass one Sunday, and she reported to our Dad we were slouching in our seats instead of kneeling up. And the faith was the normal topic of discussion in my Dad's mom's house, always with love.

My mom did not grow up in the same atmosphere. This would become one of the areas of resistance she developed within her relationship with Dad.

My brothers and I reacted differently to the division between them. Of course, we were at different ages when we experienced the same event.

But where faith was concerned, we were never encouraged to see our faith as an either-or kind of decision. Oh, I suppose on some level the teaching if you sin you will go to hell registered with us.

But the emotional turmoil, more for some of my brothers than for me, kind of diluted the impact of the message.

RONDA:

So, what would a new beginning for me look like?

I would have to renounce the fight or flight options in favor of being loving!

"Fight" equals trying to persuade everyone to think and act the way

I do concerning such matters as being Catholic (most of them are not practicing – some are not Catholics at all).

Now this doesn't mean to stop witnessing to the truth in words, only not doing so in a harsh, judgmental tone.

Given my pro-life convictions, it would be a new beginning to stop trying to influence them about who to vote for, or, at least, only in a soft tone.

DAVE:

Fr. Tom Carleton, a pro-life mentor in Boston, used to remind us that we shouldn't add to people's misery as they are coming out of the clinic after an abortion. Refer them to Rachel's Vineyard (a fantastic healing ministry for women and men who are suffering from guilt after killing a baby).

RONDA:

You know, Dave, I did sidewalk counseling and prayer for many decades. I was thrilled when Rachel's Vineyard began.

DAVE:

During the years I was sidewalk counseling in Boston, I was invited by Rachel's Vineyard to report on the experience of the mothers and fathers who made the retreat. Of course, strict anonymity was followed.

I wrote a poem:

Harvesting Voices of Hope

"Blown by the wind, her jet-black hair so flowed,
Her pretty pixie face sparkled and glowed.
Sitting on a couch, engaged in her thought
you wouldn't think her insides were so taut.

Speaking of her kids and volunteering
you're caught up in her sheer persevering.
Like a woman who you might be extolling . . . .
If you knew, you would be consoling.

He was so familiar and so warm to pull tight.
Close my eyes . . . the dance of romance . . . . so right.
In the morning, birds singing on light spring air.
A pregnancy test … she sinks in despair.

He does the thing now expected of him.
Their act is not just done on a whim.
Marching past people praying and pleading . . .
They shut down their minds and stop believing.

Years now pass but the ache never leaves.
She cannot forget a life she conceives.
Waking up, she'd sit up and speak to her child . . .
And fall back bitterly, unreconciled.

And then Rachel's Vineyard's work crossed her path.

She'd suffered through her private aftermath.
She'd searched cemeteries for her lost soul.
In her dreams, she'd see her prancing sweet foal.

In thunder and lightning inside her mind . . .
God sought with His love, her soul to find . . . .
The music she heard, she could not deny.
She had to give Rachel's Vineyard a try.

She's your neighbor sitting beside in a pew.
1/3 of the ladies are secretly blue.
Mother Mary looks upon them with love.
Sun's rays are streaming from heaven above.

At the next crash of thunder join me in prayer.
The song of dear Rachel might ease the despair.
And heal the broken soul of a woman you know.
Pray the thunder might touch where love could grow.

And then beg for rain, the rain of the voices
whose suffering bleeds from all the wrong choices
Of mothers and fathers deceived and denied . . .
Truth.

.........Lightning strike, raise these voices ... elovetrified."

Ronda, this is so ironic that this poem should come up as we write this chapter. I am reminded that God makes use of our sufferings.

For, when I was a little boy, my youthful observations of my mom in her pain might have formed in me some understanding of the sufferings endured by a mom or dad who had killed their babies.

My late brother, Dan, during the time I was working with Rachel's Vineyard disclosed in tearful remorse that he was the father of two dead babies. I had known each of his girlfriends. He said with tears, "I conceded that this was the mother's body and not my body and therefore her decision." Fifteen years later, he still had deep sorrow over the loss of his children, and so I participated in the Rachel's Vineyard weekend as the uncle of an aborted niece and an aborted nephew.

Ronda, it is chilling to remember Fr. Paul Marx's words, "We play with sex and kill our babies."

RONDA:

How poignant! My husband, Martin, whose first wife had aborted their baby, wrote a play entitled Born/Unborn to get across the father's side of this tragedy. (You can find it at En Route Books and Media.)

Getting back to fight or flight as reactions to not being able to control the family, I realize that in a new beginning, I can't rush into flight in the form of thinking I need to simply cut off any of them who disagree with me sufficiently.

Loving them, instead? I do love all of them, already. I mean 'love' in the sense of appreciating each one's unique preciousness as Dietrich Von Hildebrand defined it. (See *The Heart.*) Each one of them has amazing virtues I praise them for often.

The love that I need more of would be that forbearing love St. Paul writes of.

And 'forgiving' love.

Forgiving them for not being just like me in my good points!
Forgiving them for not doing what I know is right for them!
Forgiving them for tiny slights!

As I was pondering this matter, I found this in the Office of
Readings:

From a sermon by Blessed Isaac of Stella, Abbot

The pre-eminence of love

"Why, my brethren, are we so little concerned with finding
opportunities to advance each other's salvation, responding to greater
need with greater help and bearing each other's burdens? This is what
St Paul advised: *Bear one another's burdens and so fulfil the law of
Christ* – or, again, *forbearing each other in love.* For that is most
definitely the law of Christ.

When I notice something wrong in my brother that cannot be
corrected – either because it is inevitable or because it comes from
some weakness of his in body or character – why do I not bear it
patiently and offer my willing sympathy? ... Could it be because there
is a lack in me, a lack of that which bears all things and is patient
enough to take up the burden, a lack of the will to love?"

DAVE:

Ronda, I think you have opened up the stream of awareness I need to explore more deeply. Thank you.

In the past, when someone shares their troubles with me, my usual response has been to try to fix them. A new beginning for me could be to bear another patiently as they tell me their sufferings. And offer my willing sympathy.

Your reference to being forbearing triggers in me deeper reflections about the times I am impatient when another person complains.

Getting back to my story, my parents divorced in my freshman year of college. The battle was tough on us kids. There was real anger, meanness even between my mom's family, defending her, and my dad. My dad was overwhelmed as was my mom. One night she misunderstood my dad's decision to go to the drugstore for cough medicine, and she made a terrible mistake and got into her car to go to his office. She had a terrible car accident.

Broken hearted, my dad reached out to his mother-in-law. He and my mom had realized that not only had she injured herself, but that her drinking completely fouled her thinking. The time had come for them to separate.

RONDA:

How terrible! Didn't this increase your problems with fear, Dave?

DAVE:

As a matter of fact, the following summer I fell into my first deep depression.

I was a freshman at Boston College at the time my parents separated. Mom had decided to move to California to live with her mother. Mom stayed at her brother Ed's house in Boston before flying to California. I would see her then, in 1970. But I would just see her two more times before she died. Once, when my nephew was born in 1971, and once when I stayed with her in August 1974 at her apartment in Long Beach. She died of complications from diabetes in March, 1975.

I recall in the summer of 1970, after BC closed with student strikes which were rippling across the nation, I stayed at BC because I wanted to understand what was happening with my friends. I tried marijuana for the first time. I did not smoke much. In fact, I might have tried hash once or twice and was present when some people did lines of coke, but I was not into drugs.

For the Reader:

What was your family like when you were growing up?

Were there control or fear issues in your childhood?

If so, how did they affect your own adult life.

How would you describe efforts of yours to control family

members now?

If you love family without trying to control, describe why you are better at this than others you know.

12.

BEING LOVING VS.
TRYING TO CONTROL THE FAMILY II

"Why are you in despair, O my soul? And why are you disturbed within me? Hope in God for I shall again praise Him." (Psalm 43:5)

DAVE:

To continue with my story, the summer of 1970, I was invited to Cranwell to be a camp counselor by a Jesuit scholastic who had been a friend during my undergrad days. As a graduating senior, I had been named the George Simon award winner for Interest in Underclassmen at Boston College and he remembered.

But, that summer at Cranwell, I suffered my first real depression. I stayed at camp, came home, and prepared for and returned to BC. But I was listless. I skipped classes, wandered the streets, distanced myself from my friends, and left school on the day before I would have officially flunked all my courses.

I went home and made a suicide attempt. My dad and brothers were alarmed. But we did not understand the resources available. I went to a few nonproductive meetings at mental health clinics but largely just gradually came out of my funk.

My interior life crumbled during the next few years, and I fell into periodic depressions. I actually became suicidal several times and attempted suicide a number of times.

Only by the grace of God am I alive to share this story.

RONDA:

Oh, dear friend, Dave, you never told me about this part of your life. Maybe because of my son's successful suicide, you didn't want to revive my memories?

Did you know, Dave, I wrote a book largely about that suicide entitled:

Weeping with Jesus: The Journey from Grief to Hope?

DAVE:

No, I didn't. I reflect on the grace of your friendship for me, I have often felt your compassion for me and the struggles I have had might be rooted in your own love for your son, Charlie.

RONDA:

A suicide counselor I saw after my son's death gave me a book detailing how inevitably parents blame themselves for a child's suicide. It helped to realize, eventually, how mentally ill he really was at the time. Manic-depressive and schizophrenic, one counselor friend told me after reading my son's final journal.

Like you, dear friend, Dave, my son hid his agonies under a joyful countenance so that all who knew him were shocked at his despairing decision.

In survivors of suicide groups, I was told it was important to look at pictures of the child from before he or she was in despair. In this way, our whole sense of our parenthood isn't locked in that one awful time of the child's death by his or her own decision:

Above is a photo of my son Charlie playing the cello.

I am thinking now, however, how much God wanted to keep you

on this earth, Dave, since he rescued you from so many moments of despair.

DAVE:

Your description of Charlie reminds me of the way I survived these many years. Inwardly, I would crumble at the slightest failure. But on the surface, I seemed fine. Still, I am sure I didn't fool as many people as I thought I did.

RONDA:

I don't want to interrupt your story, but I would like to know how your therapy worked.

DAVE:

I am glad you asked. For so many years, this part of my life was so ugly and hurtful I wouldn't talk about it to anyone. I will discuss the fruits of my therapy in a few moments. I am very open at this stage of my life. But, right now, I would like to return to my story.

My life went on with a series of failed efforts in college. I dropped out of Boston College, and the College of Insurance in NYC, but got my Associates Degree from Holyoke Community College. I was active in dramatics, a cable TV club, and had a few dates. I felt I was getting back in touch with reality.

My only counseling was a retired pediatrician my dad knew. We were in the stone ages where my illness was concerned.

I took several psychology courses and did well in them at Holyoke Community College. I made a few retreats with people my age. I recall in one of them they had everybody go into different rooms in the retreat house. I was paired with a retreat director who hammered me to tell her "how I feel" about five or six times before I got angry at her.

RONDA:

Hmmmmm! I probably have gone to some ten counselors during my life. Almost all of them helped me greatly. Thanks be to God.

DAVE:

So have I, but some were lemons, like I met at that retreat house.

I have had good counselors and, unfortunately, some bad counselors. My good experiences tend to be with people who listened and responded personally. My bad experiences tended to be with authoritarian types who wanted to control me with medicine.

So, again, back to my story, I felt better, and in 1972, I was accepted at Holy Cross College. Some of my old Cranwell friends were there. I started off really well. I was asked to be a cheerleader because a Cranwell friend remembered I had great spirit. I was and had been going to Church on Sundays. But I started falling behind in my studies, got depressed, and dropped out.

So, I returned to Holyoke where I just went to work...

In a series of uninformed new beginnings, I worked in several places, with ordinary success for a number of years. I worked in offices and did entry level jobs and gradually acquired more experience and responsibility.

My social life and interest in sports was maintained. I started running and met some good people.

RONDA:

Did the exercise help you?

DAVE:

More than I knew at the time.

I went to work at Fireman's Fund in West Hartford, CT, and completed an Agent's sons' and daughters' training program. Then I went to Boston to work at CNA Insurance Company and met up with old friends. I wrote for New England Running Magazine and even had an article published on Watkens Glen, a rock concert, in Soul Sounds Magazine.

Then, I was hired by an insurance company at a better rate of pay in Hartford and I moved to Hartford.

During these years, I stayed in touch with family and friends in the faith. I had dinner with my grandmother once a week when I worked in Hartford. She had encouraged me to find an inner-city parish with a dynamic pastor. And I did!

Father Joe Looney, an Irish priest from New Haven, was pastor of St. Justin's parish on Blue Hills Ave in Hartford.

At St. Justin's, I was a lector, in the Bible Study, on the Finance committee, and sang in the choir. I made several friends in this inner-city parish.

Running in the streets of Hartford became great fun. I met active and interesting people. I even coordinated running clinics where I worked. We brought in coaches, athletes, and medical people from Boston to share their expertise with folks in Hartford.

Pretty heady stuff, Ronda, but fun! At least, until my depression started reoccurring.

It wasn't long before I was in trouble.

I actually sank pretty fast. In November, the Lieutenant Governor of Connecticut came to my Beacon Street apartment because his secretary was running a voting precinct out of my apartment.

And in April, I was attempting suicide in the same apartment.

This time, I was hospitalized for several weeks. And, finally, I acquired excellent professional help. Dr. Tom diagnosed and treated my depression with meds and encouragement to exercise and socialize. I began to get back on my feet.

RONDA:

Was this last phase you just described before your marriage or after?

DAVE:

This was several years before my marriage. I was getting back on my feet and resuming social life.

In time, I resumed dating and met a wonderful woman. We fell in love and after a fun courtship, we were married. We had a wonderful honeymoon and truly enjoyed our early years of marriage. But then I had a relapse.

Dr. Tom moved to North Carolina, and I was referred to Dr. David. My relapse to depression might have been triggered because my wife and I would have cocktails while preparing dinner. My cocktail of choice was a Manhattan, but I think the alcohol may have triggered my depression.

I had started seeing Dr. David, a new doctor, and he recommended a brief hospitalization. He tested and diagnosed me as being bi-polar.

RONDA:

Sigh! Before my son's suicide, the psychiatrist recommended institutionalization. Since he didn't want to go, we would have had to put him a straight-jacket to get him there. Because he was such a fan of the movie *One Flew Over the Cuckoo's Nest,* he refused to go to such a place. He pleaded that he was sure he was going to be okay. We believed him.

DAVE:

Oh, do I understand his resistance.

In my case, immediately, the human bias against bi-polar began to take a toll on me. People who otherwise might have been sympathetic kept their distance. I returned to work, but my confidence was sinking. During this time, Dr. Dave would meet with me in public on spring days on the lawn near the center of town. I was uncomfortable with this, and we did return to his office.

My wife and I moved out of our apartment and bought a house, partly with an inheritance from my dad who had passed away.

During this time my wife became interested in sharing our faith life. Although she was not raised Catholic, she became interested in the Bible Study at St. Justin's our parish, where we were married. Soon, our pastor asked us if we would coordinate the RENEW program in St. Justin's. We said yes!

RENEW was a small group diocesan sharing created by a priest from New Jersey to revive dialogue between parishioners. We had several groups of six parishioners at St. Justin's who met for about ten weeks. My wife and I were involved in two semesters at St. Justin's before we moved to the suburbs.

Soon we were in RENEW again in Glastonbury.

Then, one night when Fr. Joe from St. Justin's had dinner with Gail and me at our house a bright idea popped into my mind. Why not share the dialogue between parishioners of St. Justin's and St. Paul's. We would host and then coordinate two seasons of RENEW between an inner city and suburban parish!

And, so, we did.

But then God had a bright idea. We became pregnant, and soon our dear beautiful son was born.

But, unfortunately, work pressures were increasing for me. I did not manage well. So, thinking a new position might help, I sought one and was hired by the same company in a new position. But my adaptation was not quick enough and soon the respect I had in my old position doing work I knew well, was disappearing.

I was getting depressed, and a new symptom appeared. Anger. I actually had a fight in a locker room with a man who was needling me and, well, I was let go.

RONDA:

During the time you were in a new position was this when David was born?

DAVE:

Yes, I was working in my new position, but my memory is not clear on whether I was working at the time Dave was born or not.

David's birth was the most cherished moment of my life.

As part of Engaged Encounter, Gail and I were introduced to Natural Family Planning. Gail shared her embrace of NFP in our Engaged Encounter meetings with great encouragement to couples to try NFP. As an intelligent, articulate, professional young woman, Gail's communication about the symptom-thermal method was well-received.

When we became pregnant, we were introduced to Lamaze, so Gail and I rehearsed the work we would do together when our baby was being born.

And, so, I am blessed with this memory of being coach for the incredible woman whom I loved as she and I coordinated breathing as her labor progressed.

And, then, I was in the room when our son was born. They placed me next to the place where they would wash his brand new little body, and we looked at each other and then they placed him in swaddling clothes beside his mom, and they peered deep into each other's eyes. I don't think I have ever seen joy as I saw joy in Gail and David in these moments.

So, you can imagine our lives immediately were adapted to the thrills of being new parents.

This was the first time for either of us. I observed Gail adapting to being a mom with great love and tenderness.

I recall my thoughts included how am I going to be a good dad, but these thoughts were almost immediately quenched because whenever we looked at each other, I loved Dave and he loved me back.

So, our new little family was soon a very special place for each of us.

RONDA:

What memories your account of your baby's birth bring back for me. I was in one of the first groups of pregnant women trying Lamaze, and my husband one of the earliest fathers to be in the delivery room.

It happened the doctor was young and had never delivered twins before. So, in case there was a tragic problem, he didn't even tell us we had twins so that if you died we wouldn't be disappointed.

So, out comes baby Carla, and Martin starts taking off his mask, and the doctor says, "Don't take it off. The twin is about to arrive." And there was Diana.

Martin was so excited to have two babies for the price of one that he ran down to tell my mother who was waiting in the lobby of the hospital and hugged her so hard he broke a rib.

Getting back to you, at the hard time with your anger during job conflicts, did you think that you might have had anger problems from your childhood that were repressed?

DAVE:

What I did not acknowledge at the time was that my anger problems were spilling into my marriage and home life.

Yes. I had learned from Dr. Tom that depression is anger turned inside out. So, I knew anger toward myself and my perceived accumulated failures were the flimsy edifice upon which my self-worth was built. I could crumble and lose confidence. This was a learned behavior I started to practice in my childhood.

But, I had to keep working.

I worked a series of blue-collar jobs, delivering newspapers, working as a chef assistant in a seminary. Soon my wife was named to a position in management of a company branch in California. We moved with our son, Dave, and enjoyed some incredible years.

In the past, in Connecticut, I had become interested in pro-life work and poetry. In California, Gail and I thought it was a good time for me to finish working on my Bachelor's Degree. I was accepted at the University of Redlands, where I enrolled in American Studies and Writing.

During one semester, the Inland Catholic in the San Bernardino diocese hired me in a practicum to work as a writer.

I did several articles including fascinating interviews. Then, I was introduced by a good priest friend, Fr. William Kiefer, who had known me for more than a year, to his friend, Father Paul Marx. Fr. Kiefer prepared me to interview Dr. William Coulson and Father Paul Marx as we sat together in the rectory of St. Francis de Sales Church in Riverside, California.

Dr. Coulson's mentor was Carl Rogers. Fr. Kiefer wanted Paul

Marx to hear Dr. Coulson's story. The story was detailed in a Latin Mass Magazine. Dr. Coulson had the great burden of having destroyed an order of nuns in California. He and Carl Rogers convinced the nuns that truth was inside them, a humanistic psychological opinion, rather than Truth being on the Cross. Fr. Kiefer wanted Dr. Coulson to become familiar with the work of Fr. Marx in founding Human Life International.

As a result of these introductions I found my calling.

Pro Life work! My wife, who was not Catholic, was supportive for our work, and soon I was learning our faith from Fr. Kiefer like I had never known our faith before!

For the Reader:

Have you ever been depressed or wanted to end it all as more than a passing reaction to something negative?

If so, do you have someone to talk to about depression?

(If you have ever had suicidal thoughts or the plan to commit suicide, then please immediately seek counsel with a counselor, a hospital, or a psychiatrist. Here is the National Suicide Prevention Life-Line – 1-800-273-8255.)

13.

BEING LOVING VS.
TRYING TO CONTROL THE FAMILY III

"One thing I do, forgetting those things which are behind and reaching forward to those things which are ahead." (Philippians 3:13)

DAVE:

During these years when Dave was a baby in California, you and I met, Ronda!

RONDA:

I remember liking both of you from the get-go.

DAVE:

I liked you and Martin, also. However, the most important part of our encounters was that Gail had felt pressured to become a Catholic. You, Ronda, wanted to meet her and talk to her about the Church so she could make her own decision.

In California, I was becoming more traditional. But my wife, still Protestant, was beginning to feel uncomfortable within the more traditional circles I moved in. Our son, Dave, was attending CCD and meeting nice new friends. Patrick Madrid's wife was actually his teacher at St. Francis de Sales. I grew close to Father Louis Marx, pastor of St. Francis de Sales.

I did not know how to communicate my new enthusiasm for these new beginnings in my faith with my wife, son, or family back east! Gail's experience of these new beginnings was different than mine. For example, many of the women our age wore veils in Church. Gail saw the veil as a symbol of subservience. In her Protestant upbringing such women were referred to as doily Catholics. The thinking process for Gail was that these were women she didn't admire.

RONDA:

Problems with my way of being a Catholic have followed me for many years.

The Holy Spirit seems to nudge with thoughts like this: "Is part of the urgency of prodding family members to be strong Catholics, that you want to take pride in having been the mother, grandmother, great grandmother, of perfect people, even saints?"

Or, I see a little cartoon in a magazine. A wife is telling her husband: "I've got a bullet-pointed list of the ways I'd like you to surprise me."

The point for many parents is to stop trying to control their family vs. loving them while hoping for graces of conversion and the best possible life for them on earth.

A friend talks about how she is working on some family member. I see that there is something unloving about that expression "working" on him or her. It is as if you have made them an object instead of a free human person.

I think of some family member with whom I am in some conflict. My tendency is to rehearse a conversation in which I will nail them into the wall with the logic of my position.

DAVE:

How many times have I pre-thought what I was going to say to one or another of my family members. Sometimes, it would get to the point where they could feel me winding up, and they would turn me off.

RONDA:

What would it be like, instead, if I would first think of everything that is good about that person and say a Hail Mary for him or her? And then, perhaps, ask the Holy Spirit if any conversation would be productive.

Have I noticed that if I let go of my desire to control others, they sometimes surprise me by doing something very good I would never have anticipated? Or, surprise me by being right where I am wrong?

DAVE:

Your prayer makes so much sense for me in my own relationships with my loved ones in my family. Many, if not most, are doing good work, but sometimes I am only thinking of their shortcomings where Pro-Life or practicing the faith is concerned.

RONDA:

In several parishes with many Hispanics I learned a penitential practice which appealed to me. It entails making the Stations of the Cross on my knees from station to station without getting up in between. Sheltered-in-place because of Corona, I decided to go on a web where the Stations were being recited and sung, while I was kneeling and moving across the floor. I was too wimpy to do the full 14 Stations at a clip, so I divided this exercise into several days. The day I finished, a family member who is not practicing the faith told me that during a time of silence, God's love flooded her heart.

A spiritual counselor suggests thinking how much I *love* each one even if I don't *like* how they think or act sometimes.

I think of my own challenging teaching on marriage where I say: "First, in the 'honeymoon stage' your spouse is an idol (he or she who is so perfect as to make me happy the whole rest of my life). Then they become fallen idols. But, if you truly forgive each other in the grace of God, then you can laugh at each other's faults, seeing the other as 'a funny little creature, just like me.'

Perhaps we have made idols, at one point or another, of other family members?

DAVE:

In my Irish-Catholic family where many of us were great story tellers, the esteem in which we held members of my mom and dad's family might have sounded like they were idols to people who didn't know them. But many were people of accomplishment. Of course, the contrast of my mom's illness was an ache for me and probably for my dad and for my mom, herself. I identified with my suffering mom in not measuring up. My emotional health improved in a kind of new beginning when I began to forgive Mom in my memories. My experience of suffering stems from my experiential memory of her suffering. I begin healing when I can forgive her, understanding her struggle and letting go of the suffering I feel in the moment. In the moment of letting go I begin to feel her vibrance.

Where I live today in Rochester, NY, I have old pictures of my mom and my dad and my mom's family and my dad's family.

RONDA:

I think of how I love seeing the revolving photos from decades back that are on my screen saver. In photos, people almost always smile, so it seems as if all those family members are smiling at me with love in spite of all conflict.

It is good for me to turn all negative thoughts about any of my family into a fervent prayer for that very person.

I was led to go to Confession for all the sins of harsh judgment of family members.

Living in a family of four as a great-grandmother, I can't really imagine that I, the fifth wheel, can be the driver!

Do you have problems with passing harsh judgments on your family members?

Ronda and Family

DAVE:

Oh, do I practice harsh judgment on my family members?

Your words are like a thorn in my conscience. I do need to bring my loved ones to prayer, fervent prayer, and focus on the good they do.

But, Ronda, I have a question for you. How do we love the sinner but hate the sin and communicate the judgment of Almighty God our loved ones will face if they die in mortal sin? Aren't we taught that right is right and wrong is wrong but then have to deal with the fact that many of our loved ones do not acknowledge the one who provides the standards.

RONDA:

The Church certainly teaches that hell is real and that there will be an individual judgment of each human being at the time of death. We are to avoid dying in a state of mortal sin without repentance, hopefully with absolution from the sacrament of the anointing of the sick administered by a priest.

On the other hand, we are not taught that we have infallible judgment about the degree of guilt of other persons even when their sins are public. This is because there can be all sorts of factors which mitigate guilt even in the case of heinous sins. Also, we are not to be like the Pharisees throwing stones at others, but rather be eager to confess our own sins.

My experience is that it is most helpful with family members to speak the truth with love, but not constantly enunciate those truths, and never to speak about their sins with a look of superiority or a tone of hate.

DAVE:

This takes the edge off harsh judgment I can easily harbor. I am learning even my loved ones are the sum of their loved ones, their experiences, and the formation life has brought them. This is always different from the formation life has brought me.

To continue with my story, I would graduate from the University of Redlands with real support from my faculty advisor. But I had challenged Griswold vs. Connecticut and Roe vs. Wade in my Constitutional Law class and then my life pivoted on a fulcrum of new beginnings.

At first, my wife, immersed in her work with a dedication and determination I still respect deeply, was glad for my successes in the classroom, in my newspaper work and the good feedback she was receiving from people reporting to her regarding my work.

But my illness was manifesting and the new wrinkle of anger took on a more serious expression. Looking back, I am realizing we had arguments like my own mom and dad had when I was a kid.

Our son was just a youngster, a dear youngster who was loved and still is loved by everyone. But as an impressionable child, he was seeing his parents at odds. There was sharp division between us. Because the emotional turmoil between my parents was a struggle for me, my prayer today for my son is for him to find peace and strength in the love his mother and his father have for him.

After graduation, our family moved to Rochester, NY, when my wife received another promotion from her work. But in Rochester, our marriage fell apart.

My wife recognized my pro-life work was becoming a distraction for her in her work. Our differences overflowed into a fight. That was the last straw for her. So, she asked me to leave Rochester. Quietly, Gail said to me she was going to seek a divorce. Understanding our son, five years old, was our most important responsibility, I did not hire a lawyer when she sought a divorce. I had no interest in contentious proceedings that might impact our son as he was growing up. We both thought Dave would be better off living with his mother in their house with the same friends he had in school.

I had work to do on myself.

RONDA:

So, so, sad. It makes me grateful that in spite of lots of conflicts in our marriage we did remain together. Eventually, I was led at a charismatic prayer meeting to unconditionally forgive Martin. The years after that were the best in our relationship. I thought of it as moving from a C- marriage to a B+ marriage.

How did you survive that divorce?

DAVE:

It would take a few years. I had to restart my life from scratch.

At my brother Jim's suggestion, I worked a year as a lay minister for Providence Ministry for the Needy in Holyoke. Working in homeless shelters, soup kitchens, and serving as volunteer staff gave me plenty of time to sort through my wounds.

It would be a few years while I worked in student loan collections and then as an Annual Giving Officer. But I was over my wounds.

Then, a middle-aged man, I suffered the climatic depression that would spur me to recovery.

I failed at a job doing fund-raising for a pro-life leader I admired and still admire. I became despondent, sought help, and was hospitalized. The people in the hospital provided me a ladder to recovery I shall always be grateful for.

At the same time, Providence introduced me to a new therapist who, as a Franciscan University of Steubenville Graduate, understood our faith and the scientific functions of the human mind.

I was familiar with this university from my year as a volunteer for Human Life International. As a matter of fact, I applied for and was accepted to attend the graduate school of theology at Franciscan University. But, from my student loan collection perspective and my age in my early forties, the prospect of repaying $50,000 in student loans made me realize that graduate school was not in the cards for me.

My new therapist, as a Franciscan grad, understood the relationship between our spiritual life and the bio-chemical basis, particularly in the brain, where confused emotions set up thinking patterns that can lead to depression.

So, on release from the hospital, I joined a group of bi-polar and depressed people in a meeting hosted by a man who is now my Jewish 'half-brother.' I attended this group for eight years and learned so much from a resourceful, wounded, real gathering of people.

My therapist early on recognized my bi-polar syndrome was

manifested in ideas of reference and flight of ideas. Occasionally in pressured speech.

RONDA:

What is pressured speech, Dave?

DAVE:

I just mentioned flight of ideas. Imagine in your mind thoughts flying so fast you spoke fast as you would to try to get them all out at once instead of the normal rhythm in your voice. A trained observer would recognize your speech patterns as a manifestation of pressurized speech. Nowadays, I occasionally fall into such speech, but less often.

A Connecticut psychiatrist helped me with meds and met with me regularly to keep me on the right road. My therapist is a true blessing. We have been together for more than ten years now.

The winter of my discontent in my interior would be reflected in an odd way by one of the toughest winters that year in Connecticut.

Inside my little mobile home there were images of my faith including statues, paintings and a crucifix on the wall beside my bed.

In my darkest times, I could turn to Jesus on the crucifix and ask Him to give me strength in my pain. This was the genesis of a new beginning. The good therapies, counsels, and support were beginning to root in my open mind for one of the first times in my life.

From my therapist and from my group, I have gradually learned the mindfulness practices to manage my symptoms. I know, Ronda, I will always have them. But I am learning to accept them, to reach out if needed, and to work regularly to tweak my behaviors as we travel forth in time.

My Little Mobile Home by the Sea

RONDA:

Dave, so you were making progress in your therapy, and he was helping you find direction from your faith. And this helped your thinking to become clearer.

One of the reasons you and I became friends, Dave, is because I, also, have a long history of help from the combination of the wisdom of psychological counselor with deep spirituality. It saddens me that some Catholics with whom I have much in common theologically have a dislike of even Christian psychology.

DAVID:

My faith journey deepened as my peace from a psychological point of view has become better rooted. I have fallen in love, for nineteen years now, with the Traditional Latin Mass. I just made my Consecration to St. Joseph.

I live close to my son, and we are building on the love that sustained us all these years. Peace in my emotional and spiritual life is preparing me to enjoy my son.

Dave worked hard on our relationship, and so did I. And, now, we are learning from each other in the most fulfilling ways! My son's compassion and care for his wife, his students, and his friends are expressed in great love and enjoyment. Now that I am in his circle, I find his peace with me and with others is rubbing off on me.

Myself and my Son, Dave

RONDA:

Thanks be to God for the blessings you have told me about now in more detail than I heard before.

I know quite a few people who have had such painful mental problems from an early age. I find that as they heal they become tremendous witnesses to others with similar problems.

Also, because of this crucial new beginning in psychological health, the idea that new beginnings are possible is so real to you.

For myself, before closing this last family chapter in *Always a New Beginning!*, I am thinking of that 'sharp as a dagger' line from the poet Auden:

"Thou shalt love thy crooked neighbor with thy crooked heart."

DAVE:

I have trouble with that image. Do you remember *The Christmas Carol* by Charles Dickens? For me, Scrooge is a man with a crooked heart.

RONDA:

I see what you mean. For me, the line forces me to see that I can't wait until I am a saint before trying to love others. And, especially that it is not because others have crooked hearts that we don't get along so well. I do, also.

DAVE:

Now I am realizing I can have a crooked heart myself when expecting others to bend to my will.

RONDA:

I ponder such wisdom as applied to family love and I feel stuck.

Then, Jesus seems to speak to my heart with unexpected advice. For instance, before taking a nap I was in a discouraged mood about all of this. It seemed as if Jesus asked me:

"Are you afraid that if you weren't a drama queen you would be bored? Do you think the peace I offer you would be boring? My peace isn't boring, it's vibrant."

"Hmmmmmm"

I woke up in a state of rapturous peace.

Now this has happened before from time to time and I know it doesn't last, but this time I thought – is Jesus offering me His peace, albeit in the midst of the usual problems of life and real crosses, as a New Beginning?

For the Reader:

Have your problems in the work place impacted your family?

How have divorces, your own or of other family members, hurt your family?

Have support groups helped you or family members?

By contrast, have you ever done the work on yourself that could result in easier relationships in your family or in your work place?

A very helpful resource for family problems is called Healing of Memories. If you google Healing of Memories you will find many forms of this program. A favorite is the one by the Linn brothers.

You might write a letter or card to each family member saying what you love about them or describing treasured memories.

14.

RETIREMENT: A NEW BEGINNING
DAVID DOWD

"Amasias said to the man of God: What will then become of the hundred talents which I have given to the soldiers of Israel?

And the man of God answered him; the Lord is rich enough to be able to give me much than this." (2 Chronicles 25:9)

(Note to Reader: Because this chapter is the last one led by Dave followed by the last chapter led by me, they are longer than most previous chapters. You understand by now neither of us runs out of words.)

DAVE:

Now, totally retired, I can spend even more time when I am in Florida on pro-life. Each time I participate I think, before I leave this earth, I have an opportunity to help save one more baby.

One day, I was praying with friends at 'Woman's World Medical Center,' an abortion clinic at 13th and Delaware in Fort Pierce, Florida. A black truck with two people inside pulled into the dirt parking lot of the old run-down residence where babies are killed.

Parking Lot where Truck was Parked

Something about the two people sitting and talking inside the truck, parked beside the garage in this photo, struck me. I realized the baby is in the mother's womb as the man and woman talked inside the truck. A poem occurred to me.

We prayed for the unborn

We prayed for unborn babies in mom's womb.
Whose death inside this clinic was too soon.
Theirs would never meet their mother's eyes.
Her ears would never hear her baby's cry.

A black truck parked inside the parking lot.
Inside two people sat and then they watched.
See life inside the truck but not the womb?
The baby lives inside a deadly tomb.

The engine idles as the truck sat there.
Inside the truck, the two hear the engine the sound.
And babies listen to their mom's heart sound.
There's suction as the engine roars to life.
But suction of the baby means endless strife.

RONDA:

I urge the reader to go back at least twice over that poem of yours since I didn't quite get it at first. But, then, wow!

Your poem, Dave, brought back many memories of some twenty years of side-walk prayer and counseling outside abortion. In the two most recent cities where I have lived there are no open abortion clinics – though women still drive from an hour away to get to a place where their babies will die.

This meant, for me, a new beginning in pro-life work. For so many years I stood with prayer warriors on the sidewalk in front of abortion clinics. Now, in my new beginning, I can only I pray at home and give donations to pro-life groups.

But the drama queen part of me finds it hard to express my love for the babies and for the confused women having abortions, only in this seemingly less direct way by making donations to Pro-Life causes.

DAVE:

But, Ronda, what we see on the sidewalk a life and death decision being played out by every woman walking into the abortion clinic, this is not drama, this is real life. Every woman is about to have her own baby killed. Our empathy as human beings is stirred by our prayerful pleading for the baby's life and the mother's freedom. Each mother is gripped as a prisoner of sin as she walks on the sidewalk in front of us. Most times she cannot even hear us.

RONDA:

That's what I mean, Dave. When I used to stand outside these clinics every Saturday morning, I felt that it was highly meaningful to be there. But, now, when there is no nearby clinic, wanting to go out of town and block a clinic and be hauled off to prison is what seems drama-queen like to me.

Sometimes, I have fantasies about taking a taxi to one of these killing centers and blocking the door by myself, without any group support, and going to jail.

What stops me is the thought that it would only be a drop in the bucket. Also, I might go crazy in the prison with all the liabilities of an 83-year-old. Would I be doing it for drama-queen motives? As in how dramatic can you get being hauled off to prison vs. mailing a donation check?

When Operation Rescue first started, with the plan to block the doors of abortion clinics, we were told by the leaders that if their husbands didn't want them to, women shouldn't decide to risk going to jail. It would be too hard on the husbands not to be able to protect us.

What do you think, Dave? Now as a widow, should I re-think such a dramatic gesture?

DAVE:

No! Ronda, I cannot endorse such an action. To allow your mind the freedom to see yourself, offering up yourself, and risking jail for the babies can be a prayer for the babies. Even if you never do it.

Do you think Our Lord sees this prayer?

But, more important, possibly, do you think the devil is frightened by this prayer?

We need to remember something I've heard from you: "Our saints were blessed with battlegrounds with the devil in their thoughts, as they report in their writings." I think of Padre Pio and St. John Vianney. We, of course, are not them.

But let me tell you about a couple of men I met in Ft. Myers in early March.

I met Ray and Jim, quite fortuitously, one day while I was in Fort Myers to watch my beloved Boston Red Sox in Spring Training.

Our introduction was interesting, for this reminds me we always should be mindful for a new beginning to crop up in our lives.

I rented a room in Port Charlotte, Florida. The evening I arrived, an email from a friend in Rhode Island arrived with tragic news.

Rhode Island Pro-Life Leader Chris Young suffered a heart attack and died. He and his wife, Kara, and their 6-year-old daughter, Mary, had just been recorded, on a YouTube, testifying before a Rhode Island State Legislative sub-committee.

I had watched as Kara, then Mary, and finally Chris pleaded

eloquently for the committee to release the 'Heartbeat' Bill out of committee so the House of Representatives could make a public vote on the bill.

Chris, a veteran pro-life leader well known to the legislators, made a particularly key point. Time after time, he powerfully articulated this reminder.

"You will be held accountable at your final judgment for the vote you cast," he said, often emotionally.

In the family car, on their way home (Kara would later report), "Chris suffered a medical event. Kara tried to get control of the car. But the car flipped completely over and ended up with wheels back on the ground."

Kara and Mary suffered minor injuries and were treated at the hospital and released. But Chris could not be resuscitated.

Bill Cotter would publish an invitation to support Kara and Mary in the OR-Boston newsletter. He wrote, "It would be very fitting that we honor this man with alms as well as words."

But as I sat in Port Charlotte where I had intended to see the Red Sox, I made up my mind to go to Mass the next morning.

After that Mass, as I departed Church, a man who had served at the altar happened to be leaving at the same time. I asked his prayers for Chris and Kara and Mary. He directed me to the parish office where I could obtain a Mass Card.

There I saw the priest who had just celebrated the Mass. I was moved to seek his prayers.

Father Philip Schiffer invited me into his office where he solemnly listened as I related the story. Then, he cordially asked me a few questions. Then, to my surprise, he invited me to come back the following day.

The Bishop of the Diocese of Venice, Bishop Frank Dewane, would be celebrating Mass at St. Charles Borromeo Church in Port Charlotte and leading a Pro-Life Procession, on the parish grounds.

As I walked from the parish office, this series of events played out dramatically in my mind. Anticipating seeing the Red Sox play baseball at Spring Training, my life here in Ft. Myers had just changed.

The tragedy in Rhode Island turned me to prayer and the decision to attend Holy Mass. Attending Holy Mass was the pivot on which I met this extraordinary priest and now I would be joining in a Pro-Life Procession with the Bishop and the school children the next day.

My little room was less than a mile from St. Charles Borromeo Church and School!

I think Chris Young is going to become a powerful intercessor for us in the Pro-Life Movement!

Speaking of New Beginnings!

Later that afternoon, I did go to watch the Red Sox play the Twins at Jet-Blue park, but now I returned to Port Charlotte and prepared to go to Holy Mass in the morning.

RONDA:

The reader would love to know about your wonderful book of poetry called *Love, Life, Family and the Boston Red Sox.*

DAVE:

Thank you. It is a book of poetry including my baseball, running, football, and sports' poetry as well as my pro-life and other poems.

At Jet Blue Park an idea my son and I had would be hatched. David had recommended I cheer for the rookies. This idea appealed to me. So, I not only cheered for the rookies, but the next time I went back to the stadium I interviewed and took pictures of fans for their reaction at being at Spring Training in this year.

I posted my story and photos on my Facebook Page and shared this with some folks and included some new poems.

These poems can be read by you in my new book of nature poems *Reflections.*

RONDA:

So, David did you see that Bishop celebrate Holy Mass?

DAVE:

Yes, Bishop Dewane celebrated Holy Mass before a packed Church full of parishioners and the entire student body and their teachers of the parish school. Then, on the bright sunny morning, he led the Procession around the Church. And he personally circulated through the faithful offering his words of encouragement to many folks.

Following Mass, at a reception in the Church hall where we were invited for refreshments, I remembered the young Steubenville priest at St. John of the Cross in Vero Beach, Fr. Brian Campbell, where I weekly attend the Traditional Latin Mass, had encouraged us to be more social with fellow parishioners. So, in another new beginning for me, I went up to each of the tables to listen to the stories people might share and to provide encouragement.

At one table I met Silvia Jimenez. She had worked with Human Life International and is a tireless worker as the Diocesan Coordinator for Project Rachel in the Diocese of Venice, Florida. We immediately connected since I had volunteered for Human Life International and attended four Love, Life and Family Conferences.

We talked and agreed to attend Mass at The Resurrection of our Lord parish in Fort Myers on Sunday. There, Sylvia would introduce me to an excellent priest. Father Romanowski, a Fraternity of St. Peter priest, who celebrated the Traditional Latin Mass.

Following Mass, Sylvia invited me to meet some of her friends.

I followed her through the neighborhoods of Fort Myers to an elegant old house where Ray and his friend, Joe, lived.

Ronda, Joe was visiting from Eastern Pennsylvania where he and his wife manage a Divine Mercy retreat center. Ray, in his retirement, manages several apostolates in the Fort Myers region.

They are both, 'off the grid,' with no internet, no TV, no newspaper delivery!

RONDA:

I've also met some interesting people.

I know a retired air force lieutenant who decided to drop TV and internet, finding them to be addictive distractions from prayer and face-to-face encounters.

Many home-schoolers do without TV and internet or limit it greatly.

DAVE:

I am interested in the new happenings in your life.

RONDA:

A new beginning for me is to read memoirs at the public library A-Z. What I felt led by the Holy Spirit to do is to read memoirs of people whose experiences I have never known much about.

I joke that I am trying to get a 'God's eye' view of the world before I leave it.

Often, I find that a memoir helps me overcome a false understanding on my part coming from ignorance.

For example, I get into arguments about immigration policy. So, I took out a memoir called *From the Line to the River* by Francisco Cantu.

This Mexican ancestry political science student realized that he would never be able to find solutions to the border problems just by reading books and articles. So, he decided to join the Border Patrol and see for himself. He is a wonderful writer.

He gets across in a way I have never fully understood the horrible problems of good immigrants who want to escape from poverty and crime in Mexico by coming here with all the illegality problems. An undocumented worker who has been in Arizona near the border for ten years feels impelled to go back to Mexico to be at his mother's deathbed. He knows that he might not be able to get across the border to come back to his wife and kids. Even though he has a spotless record here in the US and is a good evangelical Church goer, he can't legally get back in from Mexico after going back to be with his mother in her last days. He keeps trying to cross the border with the murderous, thieving coyotes demanding ransom from his wife to try to get him through.

DAVE:

The courage that animated a soul like his stops me in my tracks. His 'front-line' reporting provides a real glimpse.

Plato says we see pictures on the wall of a cave but we need to step out into the reality.

Francisco Cantu provides us a glimpse at the reality.

RONDA:

On the other hand, Cantu, as the border control agent, details what the murderous, sadistic, addictive-drug cartel wars are like in Mexico. Much worse than I ever knew. He describes femicide, as it is called, where cartel groups seduce young women, gang rape them, and murder them chopping up their bodies into parts.

DAVE:

The base side of human nature seems to know no limits.

In an article I wrote for the Diocese of San Bernardino Inland Catholic, I interviewed a retired advisor to the National Coalition Against Pornography. He detailed the corruption taking place in a human being as the mind becomes addicted to pornography.

The corruption becomes more serious as one seeks satisfaction in soft pornography through a series of degradations ending in violence. Your description of femicide might have some kind of source in a different addiction.

RONDA:

Yes, in this case primarily drug addiction.

So, of course, we don't want to have open borders for such evil men to come in to our country at will!

I was finding this memoir so informative. Then, I suddenly realize that this same writer has not said a single word about abortion!!!!

Another memoir that amazed me was about the life of a homeless black street musician. And another about a teenage girl so neglected by drug-addicted parents that she could only survive by herself stealing and living in doorways!

DAVE:

Street musicians are common in some larger cities like New Orleans, Boston, Los Angeles, and even Savannah.

When I street preached in Boston, we met many street musicians. Some appeared homeless. Last September, in Savannah, Georgia, I stopped to watch a black street musician playing Beatles' music in one of the beautiful parks on a brisk summer day.

But many times, haven't we stood and prayed on the sidewalks of abortion clinics and possibly seen teenage girls in the same kind of desperate straits you read about.

But, Ronda, I need to return to my new beginning in Ft. Myers, Florida.

Retired Life can be so agreeable!

Jim and I standing before Our Lady of Perpetual Help

We gathered in Ray's backyard. In a far-ranging introduction, I became acquainted with them. Silvia, Ray and Joe rearranged the furniture in my mind!

These are three Catholic souls thriving on the inspired study they share with each other and friends.

Just one example:

Ray shared this quote from St. John of Avila. Ray said St. John's charism is wisdom. He is a Doctor of the Church.

"If God dwells in us, we are to restrain our feelings and make them subservient to God's will," he said.

Then we discussed his original analogy.

Ray compared our EMOTIONS to a powerful wild horse, our INTELLECT to a saddle, and our WILL to a bit!

He added, "By self-control, the small rudder guides the will."

RONDA:

I find that whereas some people are strong on intellect and will, they are poor on the good emotions of the heart such as affectionate love, adoring love of God, and delight in friendship.

However, you, Dave, have always seemed to me well-balanced on these three – intellect, will, and heart.

DAVE:

The wild horses of my emotions are not so well-balanced. I have to battle the way my thoughts and feelings arising out of my lower passions can blunt my mind.

Ray's comment to me provided me with effective new tools, if you will. I have placed my saddle on the horse and consciously pulled back on the bit if the horse wants to gallop.

But our conversation in Ray's back yard took on a new direction.

"Healing," he said, "is voltage!" As our thoughts are less entangled by disordered emotions or desires, we feel more energy!

A few days later, I was talking on the phone with my friend, John

Tuturice. John is an investment advisor for a large bank. But he has acquired his masters in philosophy from the seminary where you taught, Holy Apostles College & Seminary, through their distance learning program.

RONDA:

I remember meeting John Tuturice with you. We had burgers together. You readers might want to check out the distance learning program at Holy Apostles College and Seminary which includes A.A., B.A., and M.A. programs. See https://www.holyapostles.edu

DAVE:

You recommended Peter Redpath to be John's Thesis advisor for his Masters in Philosophy!

Now, John is working on his Masters in Theology. And he came up with an interesting point.

He said, "We want to develop an anchoring process in our interior movement (and not the exterior as in the world)." He went on, "This orients the mind so the will can be ordered toward good. The intellect sees better and prompts the mind toward good."

John offered a good adage as we sort through the demands of a given day.

"Not everything needs to be done, now."

I noted this could have a calming effect in my mind! My emotions (wild horses) tend to gallop with ideas at times! This maxim allows me to pull back on the bit and ride a little more under control in the saddle as my intellect sorts through priorities.

My emotions, as I just said (wild horses), tend to gallop.

RONDA

Aha! So, you have elevated yourself from lowly grasshopper to galloping horse?

DAVE:

No, but can you imagine the ideas of a galloping horse inside the mind of a lowly grasshopper!

John added a quip he recalled from one of his professors. When a student would ask a complex question, the professor would say, "Let's take a moment and think about this!"

"And the professor would proceed to logically, rationally and calmly review the question!" said John.

If only I could remember this bit when my wild horses are galloping inside my grasshopper mind.

Before I complete this chapter, I want to introduce a brief quote coming out of the *Introduction to the Devout Life* by St. Francis de Sales. I recently learned I could use a search engine for key terms in classics such as this.

So I did! www.catholicity.com/devoutlife provided access!

In the preface, our sainted friend, St. Francis de Sales wrote,

"Even so the Holy Spirit of God disposes and arranges the Devout Teaching, which He imparts, through the lips and the pen of His servants with such endless variety... I offer you the same flowers, but the bouquet will be somewhat different from theirs, because it is differently made up!"

Ronda, this blossomed in my mind in a funny way. You are a professor. I imagine you might have had expectations of a given classroom of students at the beginning of a semester. But this quote suggests your expectation might have blossomed in a different way as the bouquets of your students opened up!

RONDA:

In terms of new beginnings, I am finding it very different to teach the same books of mine such as *Taming the Lion Within* or *Way of Love* to a small group of women here living in a re-hab for prisoners transitioning back to the community. Among my usual philosophy students or participants in workshops, some can have a resistance to new ideas.

I believe that such a trauma as imprisonment, that these women I am teaching now go through, takes away a certain façade that most people have of conventional success. This makes them more open to learning something new in the way of Christian wisdom about the emotions and decisions.

DAVE:

I didn't know you were working with these re-hab prisoners. My late friend Allen Lyons in Connecticut and his late wife, Carol, purchased a house in New Haven as a rehab for men prisoners transitioning back to the community. This purchase, made when they were both working and their children were grown, became a burden later in life when they were on a fixed income. But, they managed this sacrifice until Carol passed away.

Interesting to me, you and Allen each brought healing to prisoners transitioning back into the community.

My friend Ray describes healing as 'voltage.' On my earlier experience with Providence Ministry for the Needy, as the men in the homeless shelter learned they could manage their routines, their confidence grew and they made better decisions.

In my wandering through the deserts of physical and psychological woundedness, I experienced deserts of dry and barrenness that challenged my sense of hope.

Ronda, as mentioned, through better nutrition, exercise and more regular practice in my spiritual life, I am experiencing voltage of my own.

RONDA:

What a new beginning! I find that I am grateful to God that working on this book together has given me more impetus in exactly those directions.

DAVE:

I noticed myself on my three-mile walk today. I was reminding myself to walk gracefully. I remembered an African champion 10,000-meter runner, gliding past me on his way to winning the Falmouth Road Race. His stride was long, but his shoulders and head and face were peaceful. This was my image of grace as I walked this morning.

My friends are prompting me to deeper study in our faith. As an unexpected bonus of meeting Ray and deepening my friendships with you and John, I felt prompted to study the "Introduction to the Devout Life" a little deeper.

I turned to Part IV, Chapter 1 (www.catholicity.com/devoutlife/4-14)

I quote, "What will you do then, my child? Look well whence the trial comes, for we are often ourselves the cause of our own dryness and barrenness. A mother refuses sugar to her sickly child and so God deprives us of consolations when they do but feed self-complacency or presumption."

Ronda, this suggests there is deeper reason behind our fasting during Lent and the Shrouding of Saints and our Lord and Lady in our Holy Churches from Passion Sunday to Easter.

Denial has a spiritual effect. I don't think I have previously understood the spiritual effect between denial and new beginnings.

RONDA:

Because I am diabetic, I was told not to fast. So, during Lent I fast from something else such as a gossip.

DAVE:

Excellent. A tough fast!

Let me end with a prayer:

"Dear St. Joseph, during my 30-Day Consecration to you, your paternal example as provider and protector in the presence of Almighty God's two most beautiful creations, Jesus and Mary, reminds me of the way you look upon life and your tasks in their daily presence.

As Ronda and I have sought through this dialogue to understand the meaning of new beginnings for us, the spiritual basis of facing my past wounds and forgiving myself and others whom I might have imagined are responsible for my wounds, free me from the burdens of self-righteous pride and self-righteous anger.

In listening to the prayers Ronda provides in conversation with our Lord and Our Lady you, St. Joseph, have set before me good example for the way you conversed with Jesus and Mary. That made me feel more new.

Just as because of Corona our atmosphere is clearing with fewer cars on the road because producing smog, calmer in my encounters sensing new freshness and alertness.

Without the preoccupations of holding on to past hurts and assigning blame, my compassionate response feels more at the ready for the encounters God provides.

In thanksgiving for the present, past, and future, new beginning. Amen"

Remembering the Benedictine motto: ora et labora, pray and work, I introduce the following meditation:

Each of us, in the service of our Lord, is a unique and unrepeatable human being. So, our bouquet, our flowers, our particular inspirations will be different from those of others persons.

But, please always help me remember the gifts you place in another person are just as important as mine.

One of the inspirational moments in my friendship with Ronda is when she described her decisions as a young woman to pursue truth.

As Pilate said to Jesus, "What is truth?" Our human nature still debates this question. Each of us might see truth from our own perspective. But from Ronda I understood her to mean that Truth is objective.

But the trajectory for your pursuit of truth is rooted in your experience, not mine.

RONDA:

Hmmmmm! That can sound contradictory. The way I would put it is that truth is objective but our journey toward it and our way of expressing it will be different.

DAVE:

Onward Christian Soldiers!
Please God may this Sheltered-in-Place time in our lives be a Pentecost moment for our faith.

For the Reader:

Please give some thought to the new beginnings in your life.

You might write down here maxims and prayers about your new beginnings.

15.

FINDING A FORMULA
OR HIDING IN THE WOUNDS OF JESUS
RONDA CHERVIN

"Their own arm did not bring them victory: this was won by your right hand and the light of your face." Psalm 43(44)

Secretly, perhaps, when I started working on *Always a New Beginning!* with my broken spiritual-warrior friend, David Dowd, I was hoping to come out of the process with a formula.

Let me explain why this can't happen. How ridiculous would it be if a warrior in battle thought that a battle cry such as 'Long Live Liberty' was enough to win the war? As if those words alone were a formula for victory.

Yet, half the e-mails I get from wonderful, strong, Catholics, run like this:

"Just say this novena for 9 days…9 weeks…and…"

The implication is that praying that novena will solve all one's problems.

Well, I write such e-mails with favorite novenas in them to my friends and followers, also!

So, then, what would be a spiritual truth to guide me in a New Beginning that would be more than a formula?

For me the truth that is becoming a guiding light comes from the famous Anima Christi prayer privately recited after Holy Communion. One of the petitions in that prayer that I have always loved is "Hide me in Your Wounds, dear Jesus."

Here is how it surfaced again while working on *Always a New Beginning!*:

A priest told me that he was getting a leading from the Holy Spirit that he was to pray for me in such a way that I would receive the final 'push' that could move me forward in my spiritual journey!

Of course, I became super-attentive to what he would say next.

He told me about a famous New England mystic who died some years ago: Eileen George, a mother of eight, who was 'brought' by Jesus on visits to heaven. The purpose was not only to increase her faith, but also to use her to give countless conferences, especially to priests, all over the world. These talks, she was told, would help priests not to lose their faith and to avoid scandalous behavior.

With such private revelations, I am cautious, but open. Most of them, such as those given to St. Faustina of Poland, or Blessed Mary Agreda of Spain, I love. Some very popular mystics I find disconcerting and avoid.

Reading one of the books of these revelations to Eileen George, I immediately noticed that it would be hard to find any mystic less like myself in personality. This mother, with no education in philosophy or theology, was a totally feminine, soft, person who calls God the Father by the affectionate title of 'Daddy.'

Nonetheless, Bishops have approved her writings.

I quickly googled her to see if there were YouTubes of her speaking. Yes, there are, and she comes across absolutely charming and delightful.

DAVE:

I think I remember when sidewalk counseling with a pro-life friend in Boston, John McCarthy, he spoke of Eileen George.

RONDA:

Now, here is the chief insight for my *New Beginning* I got from reading the accounts of Eileen George's mystical trips to heaven.

Jesus and the Father talk to Eileen in a language exactly such a woman would understand.

In the locutions I have gotten over the years, which no spiritual director has ever thought were from evil spirits, Jesus, God the Father, and the Holy Spirit talk to me in the mode of *my* understanding. When I received what amounted to booklet-amount of such locutions that I entitled *God Alone!*, they came out like short essays.

When Jesus talks to me in prayer now, often His words are kind of witty. This makes me doubt that they are from Him since His words in the Gospel are so noble.

For example, Jesus once seemed to joke with me saying: "Ronda, if you became a saint, your books would sell better."

DAVE:

This is such an important clarification.

When Jesus was speaking to Eileen George you noticed His

approach was familiar to Eileen.

But when He spoke to you, His approach was familiar to you.

This reminds me of a telephone conversation my brother Tim and I had with our maternal grandmother. When she talked to Tim she addressed him in specific words that were familiar in her relationship to him. But when she spoke to me, she spoke in words that were familiar to our relationship.

RONDA:

St. Thomas Aquinas declared that "everything is received in the nature of the recipient," as in the water you pour into a round jar looks round, but in a slim flask looks thin.

Catholic spiritual masters seem to agree that a word from the Lord takes place in a moment - compressed. Unfolding in the mind of the recipient, he or she surrounds that one message with whatever is already in that mind before.

For example, we wonder how Blessed Mary Agreda could write volumes of locutions about the life of Mary. Blessed Mary Agreda wrote during a time when the common understanding was that the world was flat instead of round. That error doesn't prove that what she received about Mary was false. Only that the purpose of the locutions were not provided to correct the science of her day, but to tell Catholics more about Mary's life!

Fast forward. Let me turn to mystical locutions put together in my booklet *God Alone*. Suppose some philosophy professor read them and disagreed with one point or another. I would tell him or her that these locutions contained ideas that are relevant for me and my readers, but not refutations of the ideas other philosophers. (If you google Ronda Chervin *God Alone* you will find out how to read these locutions for free.)

Do you see what I am getting at? Because the locutions I seem to have received don't sound like those of St. Catherine of Siena, or like those of Eileen George, doesn't mean they are not from God!

About this, Jesus seemed to tell me not to be jealous of Eileen George. These were the consoling words I heard in my heart:

"I spoke to her and brought her to heaven in the way that would reach her and those priests who would listen because she was so totally feminine. In your case, see how I gave you visions originally as a Jewish atheist to bring you into My Church and wonderful mentors, and then the Marian contemplative visions, and philosophical locutions such as *God Alone*. You will be less of a drama-queen if you are more my dedicated widow bride to whom I come with love in a unique way appropriate to your personality."

With respect to Eileen George thinking she was to call God the Father, Daddy, Jesus seemed to tell me:

"Because your father really loved you, but not in the warm affectionate way of some fathers, even though you called him, Daddy, it is hard for you call God the Father, Daddy. Now I have sent you warm fatherly figures all your life, starting with your husband."

The Holy Spirit seemed to add that since we are to become like little children, especially in the 'second childhood' of 80-year-olds, calling God the Father 'Daddy' could be for me childlike in a good way.

Daddies like to give their children surprises. It seemed as if after I tried calling God the Father Daddy in prayer that I noticed many surprises such as being called outside in yard to play badminton or unexpected words of appreciation. Or, realizing how all those smiling faces on the Screen Saver were God's gifts to me in my vocation as mother, grandmother and, now, great-grandmother.

Putting all this together, I started feeling less doubt about what seems to come from Jesus. For my *New Beginning*, I can hope that if I listen to His words to me more carefully, they can bring me to the next step in my journey toward holiness.

DAVE:

I feel like I am at a very different stage in my spiritual development.

While I recalled a Pro-Life friend in Boston named John McCarthy mentioned Eileen George, I have not paid much attention to the mystics over the years.

The mystic who spoke to Mother Angelica when Mother was a young woman comes to mind. Saint Padre Pio comes to mind.

I remember my friends in Boston speaking about Christina Gallagher.

And we discussed Audrey Santo. Audrey Marie Santo (December 19, 1983 – April 14, 2007), often referred to as Little Audrey, was an American young woman from Worcester, Massachusetts, through whom miracles were said to have happened after she suffered severe brain damage in a near-drowning accident.

A priest relative of my relative, Fr. David Joyce, was celebrating Mass in her garage when the Host turned to blood.

I have prayed to and studied the life of Padre Pio.

An Irish relative had a Prayer card to Padre Pio in his window. I visited the man's house shortly after he died.

This became a turning point in my life. I began looking at Padre Pio more deeply. Why did he make an impression on my own relative?

I did have an interior debate.

My priest mentors in California, in their discussion on private revelation, noted a difference between private revelation, investigated by the Church, such as the apparitions of Our Lady of Lourdes, and public revelation such as Scripture.

I think I have had experiences with something I thought could be private revelation.

There might have been on four occasions.

Two occurred in the Worker's Chapel, "Arch Street" in Boston where the Franciscans provided Daily Mass and Confession for working people.

These occurred during the years I was street preaching and sidewalk counseling in Boston while I worked in student loan collections.

The first occurred while prayer before the Blessed Sacrament was being offered in the lower Church.

As I viewed the Monstrance, in Adoration, the entire room seemed to turn liquid. It was as if our Lord was reminding me that He holds everything together.

This, in view of my weak faith and my struggles in life, becomes more meaningful to look back on.

The second occurred in the same Church. We used to go to Confession on Saturday before we street preached in Boston. On this particular Saturday, I came out of the Confessional and felt.... absolutely like a brand spanking new baby Catholic!

All my sins had been forgiven. My devotion to Confession has never faltered since.

The third occurred after a tragedy in my life.

My brother, Dan, took his own life in February, 2017, in the waiting area of the VA Medical Center in Greenfield, MA. He walked in, warned people they should clear the room, and used a gun.

The shock rumbled like a horrible ache for several years for me, for my son, for my brothers, and his friends.

One day, I heard Fr. Corapi on a YouTube say, God hears our prayers. Particularly, if a loved one committed suicide, we should never stop praying. God, who exists outside of time, can go back and in the instant before death, our loved one can turn to repentance.

Last summer, my friend, John Tuturice, and I went to Blessed Sacrament Church in Greenfield to make a Holy Hour.

As we walked up to the chapel, I looked up. The Franklin County Medical Center where my brother, Dan, shot himself was a few hundred yards directly behind the Eucharistic Chapel.

I remarked about the meaning of this moment for me to John. As we took our places to pray, I grabbed a rosary.

Ronda, in my 51st Hail Mary, my eyes were closed in prayer. Suddenly (and I can still see this image, now), I saw a smoke-filled room.

Then, on my 52nd Hail Mary, I saw a bullet in the chamber of a gun as the mechanism began the firing process. I saw this in slow motion.

I completed my rosary in silence. I felt as if God was revealing to me my brother did, indeed, have a moment of repentance before he died.

Dan Dowd founder of the "Cry Babies" in Greenfield, Massachusetts

RONDA:

I am not sure why you thought that vision was a proof of his repentance.

DAVE:

Fr. Corapi's encouragement to pray for loved ones who committed suicide impressed in my awareness that God, who works outside of time, can go back and provide the deceased a moment of reparation before death.

The image of a smoke-filled room followed the image of the bullet in the chamber of a gun on my 51st and 52nd Hail Mary's, where we say "pray for us sinners now and at the hour of our death" seemed to be proof of God's merciful love in answer to my prayers for my brother.

Of course, I have tried, unsuccessfully, to relate this solace to family and friends. But I do feel peace.

The fourth occasion just happened.

I made my Consecration to St Joseph on March 19 at The Holy Family parish in Piet St Lucie, FL.

I believe St. Joseph interceded in my life. He has always been part of our lives in our Dowd family. (My brother is James Joseph Dowd VII. And my son is David Joseph Dowd.)

Well, with uncertainty reigning because of the Corona Threat, I found myself responding to my son and his wife requesting I relocate from Florida to NY.

I packed, shipped boxes, and early on March 21, I departed for Rochester. Two days later, I pulled into my driveway. My son and his wife had stocked my refrigerator.

St. Joseph, I believe, delivered me safe and sound!

RONDA:

Even though such protection from the intercession of saints such as St. Joseph is not exactly private revelation, these kind of experiences of grace stay with us forever. I mean if you had a vision of St. Joseph, telling you 'leave Florida right away,' that would be what is called private revelation. Still the Holy Spirit leads us in many ways.

DAVE:

I am not sure, Ronda, I understand what many ways means here.

RONDA:

Sometimes people refer to what the Church calls private revelation as mystical experience. I often use that word mystical because of my studies of mystics such as those in my book *Prayers of the Women Mystics.* However, since some use the word mystic to refer to New Age phenomena, I use it less often.

DAVE:

This is a wonderful moment in a dialogue between friends. Your gentle re-direction of my thoughts makes good sense to me.

RONDA:

Now as I come to my closing chapter in *Always a New Beginning!*, I think the Holy Spirit could be the one flashing to me that I need to pray all day, "Hide me in Your Wounds, dear Jesus."

Spelled out further, that can be, not a formula, but the truth that I would be a holier person if, instead of blurting out whatever I think all day, and acting automatically out of habit, it would be better to center myself spiritually in the wounds of Jesus, and only do and say what I think comes out of His loving heart!

As I move forward, what are some other truths that are more than formulas?

How about insights that have come so far during the earlier work on this book?

Hasn't it been wonderful, with so much extra time due to Corona semi-quarantine, to spend much more of my day gazing out at the lake outside my living room? More time walking on the paths through the forests in the area where I reside?

DAVE:

Our Lord's timing is so awesome. In his online Traditional Latin Mass sermon this morning, Fr. Bonsignore, pastor of St Kateri Tekakwitha in Rochester, remarking on the closed churches due to Corona Virus, "It is not about place, it is about grace!"

Ronda, we are not in NYC, where you grew up, or Holyoke, MA, where I grew up. We are blessed, in retirement, to live within sight of lakes with great walking paths nearby.

I am finding life is slowing down. I am doing preparations for dinner, making healthy foods, as I never did, even in earlier retirement, when I was choosing fast food instead.

I am even driving more slowly, pulling into and away from intersections more slowly.

I am writing instead of watching TV.

My pictures and poetry focus on springtime's gradual appearances!

RONDA:

Here are some more of my thoughts from my New Beginning:

Finding a cross in my life unbearable, Jesus seemed to show me an image of Him carrying His cross and telling me that if I let Him carry my crosses with me, then they won't be unbearable.

DAVE:

Every year, on Good Friday, in Boston, Operation Rescue and Bill Cotter organize the Stations of the Cross. We process between St. Aiden's Church in Brookline, where JFK was baptized, and Planned Parenthood and the abortion clinics in Brookline.

The Procession, through Boston University and Coolidge Corner neighborhoods, moves along Commonwealth Ave and Harvard Street, two main roads in Brookline section of Boston.

One year, I was asked to carry the Cross of Christ from Preterm Women's Services at Coolidge Corner, up Pleasant St. to St. Aiden Church.

I can never forget the memory of the painful pressure in my shoulder.

And so does the idea of remaining on Pleasant Street as I literally carried the Cross!

I am reminded of these events on Good Friday this year, because long-time leader, Greg Smith, passed away, and I was writing his eulogy.

RONDA:

That is awesome about carrying the cross for pro-life.

Listing different good things I have felt led by grace to do, I find it helpful to make general confessions. This means going to a priest in the Confessional in a manner like this: I confess all the sins of anger of my whole life. I don't go into them, but wipe the slate clean once again.

Earlier in this book, I wrote about how sometimes we can use novenas as if they were formulas such that just praying this one will take away all one's problems. Novenas are wonderful, but they should express rather than replace a deep personal relationship to Jesus, Mary, and Joseph.

If I rattle through a set of prayers without consciously directing them to the person in heaven I am addressing, it is okay, but maybe a little bit like someone who says good morning to a family member without looking up from his or her iPhone.

DAVE:

I am reminded that some of our non-Catholic Christian friends observe the "by faith alone" maxim. But, as Catholics we are taught that we are also saved by our actions.

This is why I love the phrase 'ora et labora' – prayer and work, from St. Bernard.

RONDA:

Getting back to novenas, I can't end this chapter without offering you my favorite.

This one is a remedy for anxiety from a holy Italian priest who was the spiritual director of the famous St. Padre Pio: Fr. Dolindo, by name. It is called the Surrender novena.

Each day, one is to pray ten times in a row:

"Jesus, I surrender myself to You, You take care of everything."

Each day also has a paragraph coming from private revelations of Jesus to Dom Dolindo.

For example, on Day 5, Jesus tells us

"And when I must lead you on a path different from the one you see, I will prepare you; I will carry you in my arms; I will let you find yourself, like children who have fallen asleep in their mothers' arms, on the other bank of the river. What troubles you and hurts you immensely are your reason, your thoughts and worry, and your desire at all costs to deal with what afflicts you."

You can find this novena easily by googling Fr. Dolindo Surrender Novena.

I will not copy any of these out now because I would prefer to "force" you to google Dolindo: Surrender Novena and read them yourselves.

DAVE:

Ever the teacher, Ronda Chervin! Even at age 83! Involving your students by making them take action in the learning process!

RONDA:

Everyone I have sent the Surrender novena to loves it.

I also want to recommend some books written by me that readers claim changed their lives.

The Way of Love: The Journey of Inner Transformation

DAVE (interrupting)

You taught this book at Holy Apostles College & Seminary.

RONDA:

Another book that is especially helpful is

Escaping Anxiety on the Road to Spiritual Joy – co-author Albert E. Hughes.

What the Saints Said about Heaven, co-authors Ruth and Richard Ballard.

Many others you can find if you google Books of Ronda Chervin.

DAVE:

In my case, I often don't read the books I need to for my own human development.

But, when you call to mind these three books, I think I might need to be your student...

Take action!

RONDA:

From an email written by the priest who felt called to move me on further:

"Ronda, you are a joy to pray for, or better, pray with (albeit separated by distance). It's as if the Holy Spirit is moving me in the Love His Heart has and always had for you. You are beloved of Him, this I am certain. I do believe your time of suffering, your anxiousness and the sorrow of your melancholic side is turning, and the time of singing has come."

DAVE:

Blessed Mother, let this be so!
And guide dear Ronda to sing and glide gracefully!

RONDA:

That priest ends his e-mails with this beautiful quotation:

"To fall in love with God is the greatest of all romances; to seek Him, the greatest adventure; and, to find Him, the greatest human achievement." St. Augustine

Some last words seemingly from Jesus are these:

"When you know God the Father as loving as a Daddy, and I am your Bridegroom and the Holy Spirit is your Spiritual Friend and Mary your Mother, and your Angel your Protector, and all your favorite Saints your Best Friends, you will have peace. As long as you are looking for human people in these roles instead of heavenly ones you will be agitated."

Jesus continues speaking to me: "Not that I don't want you to have close friends and family, but do you see how I am gradually slightly detaching you from those you are partly using as substitutes?"

Ronda: "Why does this make me feel afraid, Jesus?"

Jesus: "You are afraid if you cling to Us you will not have the good human love you crave so much. That is not true; it will only be the purer. When you feel afraid, grab My hand and hold tight."

DAVE:

Jesus, do I get to interrupt?

We can be agitated because when we look at human people, we are looking at sinners just like us. And, we easily forget the thorn of mortal sin.

Fortunately, our faith incorporates new beginnings for our spiritual life in Christ. These new beginnings sometimes are manifest in baby steps even within our own family.

In these past few weeks, following my Consecration to St. Joseph, I have noticed my son and I often are the "protector" for one another.

I was thinking about my own dad the other day. I seem to be hearing, 'Do you remember the way your Dad spoke? His tone of voice, facial expression, his smile?'

Dear Jesus, in the Consecration, we were encouraged to meditate on scenes where St Joseph was talking to Jesus and Mary.

Dear St. Joseph, please guide me in my relationship with Dave to always be mindful of the way you spoke to Jesus and Mary.

Can Ronda and I ask St. Joseph to prompt our tones of voice, facial expression, calming influence on each other and smile?

He might be willing to help, if we ask him!

RONDA:

And just two more:

And, then I thought I need to realize that a new beginning doesn't mean that I will become like someone else. Was Teresa of Avila like Padre Pio? I will still be intellectual, funny, creative, and talkative, but less jerky, drama queen, angry, anxious, sedentary, or blurty…"

"We want you to go more 'in' and 'up' instead of 'out.'"

DAVE:

Brilliant! You are returning us to the vertical Church, Ronda!

In the name of Vatican II, the pendulum swung way too far to see our fellow human beings as the Body of Christ. For example, since Vatican II, the priest looks out at us from the altar. I love the Traditional Mass retention of the priest facing the East, called ad orientum. In this way, the priest is leading us as the people of God toward where our salvation comes from. When the priest faces us, as he does in the New Mass, he is looking at us as the Body of Christ and we naturally focus on him, a sinner like us, instead of the glory of God.

We forget He is God and we are flawed from the beginning, just dry BROKEN wood sinners!

By focusing on the horizontal relationship between people of the Church, all of us sinners, we miss the ascendancy in our relationship with Almighty God.

RONDA:

And, suppose, Dave, the best new beginning for you will be if you become one day St. David?

DAVE:

And, suppose, Ronda, the best new beginning for you will be if you become one day St. Ronda?

RONDA:

I was thinking we should take out those last two lines about becoming saints because it could sound vainglorious. Then I thought, "Heh, should we be hoping to remain sinners forever?"

And, Dave, after our souls have been seared in the fires of purgatory, shall we meet at the gates of the only true New Beginning: Heaven?

Some people think heaven will be boring, but I like to say:

"If you want to know what heaven will be like, remember the most glorious moment of your whole life – the birth of a baby of yours, a sunset over the ocean…and then multiply the joy by infinity."

"With God all things are possible!" (Matthew 19:36)

For the Reader:

Given that we are all called to holiness, how would your interior life and your life with others be different if you were guided by more saintly virtue?

Is there a prayer from your own experience, such as, "Hide me in Your Wounds," that would open you to greater virtue?

16.

AFTERWORD: FAVORITE SPIRITUAL ADAGES OF MENTORS AND FRIENDS

Continuing our new beginning, I, Ronda, thought I would "pack into my suitcase" some of my favorite Spiritual Adages from Mentors and Friends.

"Don't confuse intensity with depth." (my godfather, Balduin Schwarz)

"Mom, you are always right, but you say it in such a nasty way no one wants to give in!" (my son, Charles Chervin)

"Be more receptive." (Alice Von Hildebrand)

"Don't hard-boil others in their sins." (Julie Loesch)

"Don't start so many sentences with the word 'I'." (Fr. Dennis Kolinski)

"Every utopia becomes gulag!" (Gary McCabe)

"Be in the present in the Presence." (Fr. Mike Phillippino)

"With disagreements in the family start with 'I *love* you,' and then add if you have to that you don't *like* what they think about some topic. (Marti Armstrong)

"Non-forgiveness over many years can be a bigger sin than the sin you think you can't forgive!" (Bob Olson)

"Humor is the oil for the engine of success; for the friction of stress; and for the wear and tear of the ego." (Bob Sizemore)

DAVE:

Inspiring Quotations from Family and Friends:

From a poem of my dad for his sons:

Knowing these are precious years,
Precious ones I'll always remember.
Everything I know or own,
From my world, the best you're shown.
This, my vow, as I watch you in slumber.

(December, 1959)

From my first poem:

"America is a melting pot
Of many a race and creed."

(December, 1964)

From my dad's poem:

"It's fellowship and never anger."
"We will take the Newtons over Margaret Sanger."

(April, 1970)

Quote from my dad:

"People are as nice as they know how to be." (October, 1986)

Quote from my Dad, as I started work in corporations:

"Pas du la Rhône Canoe"

(January, 1979)

I restarted my life after my marriage ended:

"Trust the wisdom of youth,"
—— my brother, Jim. (When my marriage ended).

"Love is always stronger."
——- Shared back and forth with my son, Dave.

"Did you do 'The Work'?
—. My sister in law, Dawn

Took me a while to understand this:
(my brother, Dan, loved Johnny Cash.)

"Get a rhythm when you get the blues"

- Johnny Cash

Some quotes from Coach Bill Squires (a Marathon coach from Boston with whom I worked closely in 1980.)

"That's the thing I put into my marathon champions such as Alberto Salazar and Greg Meyer and all those guys."

"I don't tell them to do that but it's part of my coaching."

"We don't run against no talent; we go against good teams!"

"I remind them, 'Are you going to waste our time?'

"No," I say, "We're going to get something out of this race."

"I think that was instilled in me as a runner."

(Learning from Coach Bill Squires taught me the importance of learning from the best coaches. This prepared me to be open to learning from Fr. Paul Marx, Human Life International, and Chris Slattery.)

More Quotes:

Bill Cotter to Cardinal Law, "If our sidewalk counselors go back on the sidewalks to save babies from abortion, will we be committing a sin?"

Cardinal Law, "No."

(December: 1994)

Anne Smith "Smitty" Fitzpatrick:

"ProLifers are the best people in the world,"

(December: 1993)

My German teacher, Fr. John Walchars, S.J., at Cranwell, still inspires me:

"If any time reaches out for forgiveness, it is our time. If any generation begs for pardon, it is our generation. Having amassed such a heap of guilt, we need an equal abundance of forgiveness.

Sins of injustice, our utter disregard for life, the defiance of immorality, all cry out to God for mercy and compassion.

Not that our civilization is particularly corrupt – other periods in history had their share of indiscretion – But we were destined for leadership, and so far we have failed in that mission."

I love poetry:

A glimmer, and then a gleam of light!
He springs to the saddle, the bridle he turns,
But lingers in gazes, 'til full in his sight
A second lamp in the belfry burns!

from "Midnight Ride of Paul Revere"

"In Thanksgiving for the mark of Faith which characterized your ancestors."

Fr. William Crean P.P.
St. Mary's Church
Castlegregory, County Kerry, Ireland

(June, 2003)

A few from Fr. Paul Marx, OSB:

"Be good, work hard, and never give up."
(October 25, 2002)

"In your letter to meet you speak of courage. Surely, that is a much-needed virtue in these strange times in which the devil stirs up so much trouble.
(April 27, 2006)

"May the good Lord keep you in the palm of his hand, as the Irish say. And the Germans should, and know that you are always in my prayers."
(January 20, 2006)

My roommate, Sean Brogan, whenever I assumed someone's remark intentionally hurt me. "Presume they are innocent."
(August, 2006)

Chris Slattery, founder of Expectant Mother Care in New York

City, opened Save the Life Centers Rally in the rally for life in a local Bronx church. He assembled pro-life leaders from New York and across the nation.

Slattery said, "The people in this room can make a difference."

(February 7, 2011)

Bernadette Smyth, Director of Precious Life in Northern Ireland gave a talk on spiritual truths.

She proclaimed,

"The battle is the Lord's!
Why are we not afraid?
because the battle is the Lord's.
Why do we not panic?
because the battle is the Lord's.
Why do we turn the other cheek?
 because the battle is the Lord's.
Why do we have patience when we are persecuted?
because the battle is the Lord's.
Why do we stand firm?
 because the battle is the Lord'

(January 2013)

"David, I appreciate so much all you do to salvage our miserably immoral society. Keep up the great work!"

Yours for Life, Joe Scheidler. National Director, Pro Life Action League

(June 5, 2018)

From Fr Donald Calloway:

"Thanks, brother! Yes, the Church is in a major spiritual battle today. It needs to be cleansed from the top down. Tough times, my friend. Tough tough times. On another note, amazing about Fr. Seraphim. That guy is going to live forever! Would you believe he is still traveling and speaking! Blessings!

Iron sharpens iron. Together we attack the enemy. Together we stand as brothers in arms! God bless!"

(January, 22, 2020)

From Fr. John Hardon, S.J.:

"What have you done today to prepare for eternal life."

(1990: Live Life and Family Conference: Santa Clara, CA)

From my dear son, Dave:

"Dad, you are either going to do the work or not."

"Dad, if you ask questions first, the person you are speaking with might be a better listener."

"Listen, ask questions, withhold your story. Not everyone is interested."

Working with you, Ronda, dear friend, I am giving serious thought to writing my auto-biography. These adventures in new beginnings prepare me for another new beginning. I hope, my dear friend and mentor, will join me on this exciting new chapter in my life.

Made in the USA
Middletown, DE
25 September 2022

11015221R00136